Data Structures and Algorithms
100 Interview Questions

X.Y. Wang

Contents

1

4 Advanced 76

Chapter 1

Introduction

Welcome to "Data Structures and Algorithms: 100 Interview Questions". As the field of computer science continues to evolve, the importance of understanding data structures and algorithms has become paramount for professionals in the industry. These fundamental concepts are the building blocks for efficient and scalable software solutions. For students, developers, and even experienced engineers, mastering these topics is essential for success in job interviews, academic studies, and professional careers.

This book serves as a comprehensive resource, covering essential topics in data structures and algorithms through a collection of 100 carefully curated interview questions. The questions are organized into five difficulty levels: Basic, Intermediate, Advanced, Expert, and Guru. Each level delves deeper into the subject matter, providing you with a well-rounded understanding of the topic and preparing you for even the most challenging interview scenarios.

In the Basic level, you will familiarize yourself with fundamental concepts, such as arrays, linked lists, stacks, queues, binary trees, and hash tables. You will also learn about time complexity, Big O notation, recursion, and basic graph theory.

The Intermediate level expands upon the foundations laid in the Basic section, introducing more complex concepts like time and space complexity, merge sort, insertion sort, Dijkstra's algorithm, dynamic programming, and greedy algorithms.

The Advanced level covers more sophisticated topics, such as the A* search algorithm, Bloom filters, self-balancing binary search trees, B-trees, and B+ trees. You will also explore various techniques for cycle detection, garbage collection, and concurrent data structures.

In the Expert level, you will delve into the intricacies of distributed systems, deterministic and non-deterministic algorithms, data compression, locality-sensitive hashing, and parallel algorithms. This section also covers the external merge sort, Monte Carlo algorithms, and various concurrency control algorithms.

Lastly, the Guru level pushes the boundaries of your understanding with topics such as algorithmic information theory, NP-completeness, randomized algorithms, quantum algorithms, and streaming algorithms. You will also explore cutting-edge research areas like succinct data structures, compressed data structures, and algorithmic game theory.

By working through the questions in this book, you will not only reinforce your understanding of data structures and algorithms but also gain valuable experience in applying these concepts to real-world problems. Whether you are a student seeking to excel in your studies, a professional preparing for a job interview, or an experienced engineer looking to expand your knowledge, this book is the ideal resource to help you achieve your goals.

Embark on your journey to mastery in data structures and algorithms with confidence, knowing that with every question you tackle, you are one step closer to success. Happy learning!

Chapter 2

Basic

2.1 What is a data structure? Give a few examples of commonly used data structures.

A data structure is a way of organizing and storing data in a computer program so that it can be accessed and used efficiently. It provides a framework for organizing data that makes it easier to perform operations such as inserting, deleting, and searching for data. Data structures are essential in computer science because they provide a way to manage and manipulate large amounts of data in an organized and efficient manner.

Here are a few examples of commonly used data structures:

Arrays: An array is a collection of elements of the same data type that are stored in contiguous memory locations. Each element in an array is identified by an index, which starts at 0. Arrays are commonly used to store lists of items such as integers, characters, or objects.

Here is an example of how to create an array of integers in Java:

```
int[] myArray = new int[10];
```

This creates an array of integers called myArray with a length of 10.

Linked Lists: A linked list is a collection of elements called nodes, where each node contains data and a reference to the next node in the list. Unlike arrays, linked lists do not have to be stored in contiguous memory locations, and their size can be changed dynamically. Linked lists are commonly used to implement stacks, queues, and other data structures.

Here is an example of how to create a linked list of integers in Java:

```
class Node {
   int data;
   Node next;
}

Node head = new Node();
Node second = new Node();
Node third = new Node();

head.data = 1;
head.next = second;

second.data = 2;
second.next = third;

third.data = 3;
third.next = null;
```

This creates a linked list of integers with three nodes containing the values 1, 2, and 3.

Stacks: A stack is a data structure that allows elements to be added and removed only from one end, called the top. Stacks follow the Last-In-First-Out (LIFO) principle, meaning that the last element added to the stack will be the first one to be removed.

Here is an example of how to implement a stack of integers using an array in Java:

```
class Stack {
  private int[] array = new int[10];
  private int top = -1;

  public void push(int data) {
    array[++top] = data;
  }

  public int pop() {
    return array[top--];
  }
}
```

This creates a stack of integers that can hold up to 10 elements.

These are just a few examples of the many data structures that are commonly used in computer science. Choosing the right data structure for a particular problem can be crucial in developing an efficient algorithm, and it often depends on the specific requirements of the problem.

2.2 Explain the differences between arrays and linked lists.

Arrays and linked lists are both fundamental data structures used in computer programming to store and manipulate collections of data. Although they have similarities in that they both allow us to store a sequence of elements, they differ in their implementation, performance characteristics, and the types of operations that can be performed efficiently.

Here are some of the key differences between arrays and linked lists:

Memory Allocation: Arrays are stored in contiguous memory locations, whereas linked lists are not. In an array, each element takes up a fixed amount of memory, and the elements are stored next to each other. In a linked list, each element (node) has a data field and a pointer field that points to the next node in the list. Because of this, linked lists do not need to have a contiguous block of memory allocated, and their size can be changed dynamically.

Insertion and Deletion: Arrays are not very efficient when it comes to insertion and deletion of elements in the middle, especially if the size of the array is large. To insert or delete an element at a particular position in an array, all the elements after that position must be shifted up or down by one, respectively. This operation takes $O(n)$ time, where n is the size of the array. In contrast, linked lists are better suited for insertion and deletion operations because they do not require shifting elements. To insert or delete an element in a linked list, only the pointers of the nodes need to be updated, which takes $O(1)$ time.

Random Access: Arrays provide constant-time access to any element in the array using an index. In contrast, linked lists do not provide constant-time access to elements at arbitrary positions. To access an element in a linked list, you must traverse the list from the beginning until you reach the desired element. This operation takes O(n) time, where n is the size of the list.

Memory Overhead: Arrays have a lower memory overhead compared to linked lists, since they do not require extra memory for the pointers between the elements. However, linked lists can be more memory-efficient when the size of the collection needs to be changed frequently or when we don't know the maximum size of the collection in advance.

Here is an example of how to create an array and a linked list in Java:

```
// Creating an array of integers
int[] arr = new int[5];
arr[0] = 1;
arr[1] = 2;
arr[2] = 3;
arr[3] = 4;
arr[4] = 5;

// Creating a linked list of integers
class Node {
    int data;
    Node next;
}
Node head = new Node();
head.data = 1;
Node second = new Node();
second.data = 2;
head.next = second;
Node third = new Node();
third.data = 3;
second.next = third;
```

In summary, arrays are better suited for situations where we need to access elements at arbitrary positions in constant time, and when the size of the collection is fixed. On the other hand, linked lists are more appropriate when we need to frequently insert or delete elements, and when the size of the collection can change dynamically.

2.3 Can you define a stack and a queue? Explain how they differ from each other.

A stack and a queue are two popular abstract data types that are used to store and retrieve elements in a particular order. Both of these data structures have their own unique properties and are suited for specific use cases.

A stack is a collection of elements that can be accessed only from one end, known as the top of the stack. The Last-In-First-Out (LIFO) principle governs stacks, which means that the last element added to the stack will be the first one to be removed. The most common operations performed on a stack are push and pop. Push adds an element to the top of the stack, whereas pop removes and returns the top element from the stack.

Here is an example of how to implement a stack in Java:

```java
class Stack {
    private int[] elements;
    private int top;

    public Stack(int size) {
        elements = new int[size];
        top = -1;
    }

    public void push(int value) {
        elements[++top] = value;
    }

    public int pop() {
        return elements[top--];
    }
}
```

A queue, on the other hand, is a collection of elements that can be accessed from both ends. The First-In-First-Out (FIFO) principle governs queues, which means that the first element added to the queue will be the first one to be removed. The most common operations performed on a queue are enqueue and dequeue. Enqueue adds an element to the end of the queue, whereas dequeue removes and returns the element from the front of the queue.

Here is an example of how to implement a queue in Java:

```java
class Queue {
```

```
private int[] elements;
private int front;
private int rear;

public Queue(int size) {
    elements = new int[size];
    front = -1;
    rear = -1;
}

public void enqueue(int value) {
    if (isEmpty()) {
        front = 0;
        rear = 0;
    } else {
        rear++;
    }
    elements[rear] = value;
}

public int dequeue() {
    int value = elements[front];
    if (front == rear) {
        front = -1;
        rear = -1;
    } else {
        front++;
    }
    return value;
}

public boolean isEmpty() {
    return front == -1 && rear == -1;
}
}
```

The main difference between a stack and a queue is the order in which elements are added and removed. In a stack, the last element added is the first one to be removed, whereas in a queue, the first element added is the first one to be removed. Additionally, stacks are best suited for problems where we need to keep track of the most recently added elements, whereas queues are best suited for problems where we need to process elements in the order they were added.

In summary, stacks and queues are two popular abstract data types that are used to store and retrieve elements in a particular order. Both of these data structures have their own unique properties and are suited for specific use cases.

2.4   What is a binary search algorithm, and what is its time complexity?

A binary search algorithm is a searching algorithm that works by repeatedly dividing the search interval in half. It is a very efficient algorithm for finding a particular value in a sorted array or list.

The binary search algorithm works as follows:

- We first compare the target value to the middle element of the sorted array or list.

- If the target value is equal to the middle element, then we have found the value we were looking for, and the search is complete.

- If the target value is less than the middle element, we then repeat the search on the lower half of the array.

- If the target value is greater than the middle element, we then repeat the search on the upper half of the array.

- We repeat this process until the target value is found or until the search interval is empty.

Here is an example of how to implement a binary search algorithm in Java:

```java
public static int binarySearch(int[] arr, int target) {
    int low = 0;
    int high = arr.length - 1;
    while (low <= high) {
        int mid = (low + high) / 2;
        if (arr[mid] == target) {
            return mid;
        } else if (arr[mid] < target) {
            low = mid + 1;
        } else {
            high = mid - 1;
        }
    }
    return -1;
}
```

In this example, the binarySearch() method takes an array of integers and a target value as parameters. It then initializes the low and high variables to the first and last indices of the array, respectively. The method then enters a loop where it calculates the middle index of the search interval and compares the target value to the element at the middle index. Depending on the comparison, the search interval is either halved by setting the high or low variable to mid+1 or mid-1, respectively. The loop continues until the target value is found, or until the search interval is empty. If the target value is not found, the method returns -1.

The time complexity of the binary search algorithm is O(log n), where n is the size of the array or list being searched. This is because the search interval is halved with each iteration of the loop, which reduces the number of elements that need to be searched by half at each step. Therefore, the time it takes to find the target value grows logarithmically with the size of the array or list.

In summary, the binary search algorithm is a very efficient algorithm for finding a particular value in a sorted array or list. It has a time complexity of O(log n), making it a very fast algorithm for searching large datasets.

2.5 What is Big O notation, and why is it important for analyzing algorithms?

Big O notation is a mathematical notation that is used to describe the time complexity or space complexity of an algorithm. It is used to describe how the time or space requirements of an algorithm grow with the size of the input data.

In Big O notation, we express the upper bound on the growth rate of an algorithm as a function of the input size. This allows us to compare the efficiency of different algorithms and choose the one that is best suited for a particular problem.

For example, let's consider the following algorithm that computes the sum of the first n integers:

```
int sum = 0;
for (int i = 1; i <= n; i++) {
    sum += i;
```

}

The time complexity of this algorithm is O(n), because the number of iterations of the loop is proportional to the size of the input n. As n grows larger, the time it takes to compute the sum grows linearly with n.

Big O notation is important for analyzing algorithms because it allows us to make predictions about the performance of an algorithm before we actually run it. By understanding the time complexity of an algorithm, we can make informed decisions about which algorithm to use for a particular problem. In addition, Big O notation can help us identify areas in an algorithm that can be optimized to improve its performance.

Here are some common time complexity classes that are used in Big O notation:

- O(1) - constant time: The algorithm's performance is not affected by the size of the input data.

- O(log n) - logarithmic time: The algorithm's performance grows logarithmically with the size of the input data.

- O(n) - linear time: The algorithm's performance grows linearly with the size of the input data.

- $O(n^2)$ - quadratic time: The algorithm's performance grows quadratically with the size of the input data.

- $O(2^n)$ - exponential time: The algorithm's performance grows exponentially with the size of the input data.

In summary, Big O notation is a mathematical notation used to describe the time complexity or space complexity of an algorithm. It is important for analyzing algorithms because it allows us to make predictions about their performance and choose the best algorithm for a particular problem. By understanding the time complexity of an algorithm, we can optimize it to improve its performance and avoid inefficiencies.

2.6 Describe the process of recursion and provide a simple example.

Recursion is a programming technique in which a function calls itself repeatedly until a base case is reached. It is a powerful tool that allows us to solve complex problems by breaking them down into simpler subproblems. The process of recursion can be divided into two parts: the base case and the recursive case.

The base case is the condition that determines when the recursion should stop. If this condition is not met, the function will continue to call itself until the base case is reached. The base case is crucial because it prevents the function from calling itself indefinitely, which would lead to an infinite loop and a stack overflow error.

The recursive case is the condition that calls the function recursively. This means that the function calls itself with a modified input, typically a smaller or simpler version of the original input. The recursive case allows the function to break down a complex problem into simpler subproblems until the base case is reached.

Here is a simple example of recursion in Java that calculates the factorial of a number:

```
public static int factorial(int n) {
    if (n == 0) {
        return 1;
    } else {
        return n * factorial(n-1);
    }
}
```

In this example, the factorial() method takes an integer n as input and calculates the factorial of n recursively. The base case is when n equals 0, in which case the method returns 1. The recursive case is when n is greater than 0, in which case the method calls itself with n-1 as the input and multiplies the result by n. This recursive process continues until the base case is reached, at which point the final result is returned.

For example, if we call the factorial() method with n = 4, the following sequence of calls will be made:

```
factorial(4)
4 * factorial(3)
4 * 3 * factorial(2)
```

```
4 * 3 * 2 * factorial(1)
4 * 3 * 2 * 1 * factorial(0)
4 * 3 * 2 * 1 * 1 = 24
```

In summary, recursion is a programming technique that involves a function calling itself recursively until a base case is reached. It is a powerful tool that allows us to solve complex problems by breaking them down into simpler subproblems. The process of recursion involves two parts: the base case and the recursive case. The base case is the condition that determines when the recursion should stop, while the recursive case is the condition that calls the function recursively with a modified input.

2.7 What is a hash table, and how does it work?

A hash table is a data structure that is used to store and retrieve key-value pairs. It is also known as a hash map, dictionary, or associative array. A hash table works by using a hash function to map each key to a corresponding index in an array.

The hash function takes the key as input and produces a hash code, which is an integer value that represents the key. The hash code is then used to calculate an index in the array, where the corresponding value is stored. In most cases, the hash function should produce the same hash code for the same key every time it is called.

To handle collisions, where two or more keys map to the same index, the hash table uses a collision resolution strategy. The most common strategies are chaining and open addressing.

In chaining, each index in the array stores a linked list of key-value pairs that have the same hash code. When a new key-value pair is inserted, it is added to the linked list at the corresponding index. If a collision occurs when inserting a key-value pair, it is added to the end of the linked list.

In open addressing, each index in the array stores a single key-value pair. When a new key-value pair is inserted, the hash table checks whether the corresponding index is already occupied. If it is, the hash table looks for the next available index in the array using a probing sequence. A probing sequence is a sequence of indices that the hash table checks until an empty index is found. When a collision occurs, the hash table uses a variation of the probing sequence to determine the next index to check.

Here is an example of how to implement a hash table in Java using chaining:

```java
class HashTable {
    private int capacity;
    private LinkedList<Entry>[] table;

    public HashTable(int capacity) {
        this.capacity = capacity;
        table = new LinkedList[capacity];
    }

    public void put(int key, int value) {
        int index = hash(key);
        if (table[index] == null) {
            table[index] = new LinkedList<>();
        }
        for (Entry entry : table[index]) {
            if (entry.key == key) {
                entry.value = value;
                return;
            }
        }
        table[index].add(new Entry(key, value));
    }

    public int get(int key) {
        int index = hash(key);
        if (table[index] == null) {
            return -1;
        }
        for (Entry entry : table[index]) {
            if (entry.key == key) {
                return entry.value;
            }
        }
        return -1;
    }

    private int hash(int key) {
        return key % capacity;
    }

    private static class Entry {
        int key;
        int value;

        public Entry(int key, int value) {
            this.key = key;
            this.value = value;
        }
    }
}
```

```
}
```

In this example, the HashTable class implements a hash table using chaining. The class has a capacity field that determines the size of the array, and a table field that is an array of linked lists. The put() method takes a key-value pair as input and inserts it into the hash table. The get() method takes a key as input and returns the corresponding value from the hash table. The hash() method takes a key as input and returns the corresponding index in the array using the modulo operator. The Entry class represents a key-value pair that is stored in the hash table.

In summary, a hash table is a data structure that is used to store and retrieve key-value pairs. It works by using a hash function to map each key to a corresponding index in an array. To handle collisions, it uses a collision resolution strategy such as chaining.

2.8 What are binary trees, and why are they useful in computer programming?

A binary tree is a tree data structure in which each node has at most two children, referred to as the left child and the right child. The left child is typically smaller than the parent, while the right child is typically larger than the parent. Binary trees are useful in computer programming because they can be used to implement a wide range of algorithms, such as searching, sorting, and parsing.

Binary trees are used to represent hierarchical data structures, such as file systems, organizational charts, and family trees. They are also used in data compression algorithms, such as Huffman coding, where a binary tree is used to represent the frequency of characters in a message. In addition, binary trees are used in computer graphics to represent 3D scenes, where the nodes of the tree represent objects in the scene and the edges represent the relationships between the objects.

Here is an example of how to implement a binary tree in Java:

```
class Node {
    int value;
    Node left;
```

```
    Node right;

    public Node(int value) {
        this.value = value;
        this.left = null;
        this.right = null;
    }
}

class BinaryTree {
    Node root;

    public BinaryTree() {
        root = null;
    }

    public void insert(int value) {
        root = insertRecursive(root, value);
    }

    private Node insertRecursive(Node current, int value) {
        if (current == null) {
            return new Node(value);
        }
        if (value < current.value) {
            current.left = insertRecursive(current.left, value);
        } else if (value > current.value) {
            current.right = insertRecursive(current.right, value);
        } else {
            return current;
        }
        return current;
    }

    public boolean contains(int value) {
        return containsRecursive(root, value);
    }

    private boolean containsRecursive(Node current, int value) {
        if (current == null) {
            return false;
        }
        if (value == current.value) {
            return true;
        }
        return value < current.value
                ? containsRecursive(current.left, value)
                : containsRecursive(current.right, value);
    }
}
```

In this example, the Node class represents a node in the binary tree, with an integer value and left and right child nodes. The BinaryTree class represents the binary tree itself, with a root node and methods for inserting and searching for values in the tree. The insert() method takes a value as input and inserts it into the binary tree. The contains() method takes a value as input and returns true if the value is present in the binary tree, and false otherwise.

In summary, binary trees are a useful data structure in computer programming because they can be used to represent hierarchical data structures, implement a wide range of algorithms, and solve a variety of problems. They are commonly used in data compression algorithms, computer graphics, and many other fields. The implementation of binary trees can be complex, but they provide a powerful tool for solving many types of problems.

2.9 What is the difference between depth-first search (DFS) and breadth-first search (BFS)?

Depth-first search (DFS) and breadth-first search (BFS) are two common algorithms used for traversing and searching graph data structures. While both algorithms can be used to explore a graph and find a particular node or path, they differ in their approach and behavior.

DFS starts at the root node (or any starting node) and explores as far as possible along each branch before backtracking. This means that it traverses the graph depth-wise before exploring its breadth. In other words, it explores as deep as possible before going wide. DFS uses a stack data structure to keep track of the nodes to visit next. DFS is useful for finding all nodes in a graph, determining whether a path exists between two nodes, and finding cycles in a graph.

Here is an example of DFS traversal in a binary tree:

```
void DFS(Node node) {
    if (node == null) {
        return;
    }
    System.out.print(node.value + "␣");
    DFS(node.left);
    DFS(node.right);
}
```

In this example, DFS starts at the root node and recursively visits the left subtree and right subtree of each node in a depth-first order. The output of DFS traversal would be the values of the nodes in the binary tree printed in a depth-first order.

BFS, on the other hand, starts at the root node (or any starting node) and explores all the neighboring nodes at the current depth before moving on to the next level. This means that it traverses the graph breadth-wise before exploring its depth. In other words, it explores as wide as possible before going deep. BFS uses a queue data structure to keep track of the nodes to visit next. BFS is useful for finding the shortest path between two nodes in a graph, finding the minimum number of moves required to reach a destination, and finding the connected components of a graph.

Here is an example of BFS traversal in a binary tree:

```
void BFS(Node node) {
    Queue<Node> queue = new LinkedList<>();
    queue.add(node);
    while (!queue.isEmpty()) {
        Node current = queue.poll();
        System.out.print(current.value + "␣");
        if (current.left != null) {
            queue.add(current.left);
        }
        if (current.right != null) {
            queue.add(current.right);
        }
    }
}
```

In this example, BFS starts at the root node and visits all the neighboring nodes at the current depth before moving on to the next level. It uses a queue to keep track of the nodes to visit next. The output of BFS traversal would be the values of the nodes in the binary tree printed in a breadth-first order.

In summary, DFS and BFS are two common algorithms used for traversing and searching graph data structures. DFS explores as far as possible along each branch before backtracking, while BFS explores all the neighboring nodes at the current depth before moving on to the next level. DFS is useful for finding all nodes in a graph and determining whether a path exists between two nodes, while BFS is useful for finding the shortest path between two nodes and finding the connected components of a graph.

2.10   Explain the concept of a graph data structure and its applications.

A graph is a data structure consisting of a set of nodes (vertices) and a set of edges connecting them. Each edge connects two nodes and can be directed or undirected. Graphs are a fundamental data structure in computer science and are used to model a wide range of real-world systems, including social networks, transportation systems, and communication networks.

There are two main types of graphs: directed graphs (also known as digraphs) and undirected graphs. In a directed graph, the edges have a direction and represent a one-way relationship between two nodes. For example, a directed graph could represent a social network where the nodes are people and the edges represent the direction of friendships. In an undirected graph, the edges do not have a direction and represent a two-way relationship between two nodes. For example, an undirected graph could represent a road network where the nodes are intersections and the edges represent the roads connecting them.

Graphs can be represented using various data structures, including adjacency matrices, adjacency lists, and edge lists. Adjacency matrices are a two-dimensional array that represents the connections between nodes. Adjacency lists are a list of nodes with each node containing a list of its adjacent nodes. Edge lists are a list of edges with each edge containing the nodes it connects.

Graphs have many applications in computer science, including:

Network analysis: Graphs are used to model and analyze complex networks, such as social networks, transportation systems, and communication networks. By analyzing the structure of these networks, we can gain insights into their behavior and optimize their performance.

Pathfinding: Graphs are used to find the shortest path between two nodes, such as in routing algorithms for transportation systems or navigation systems for autonomous vehicles.

Recommendation systems: Graphs are used to model the relationships between users and items, such as in recommendation systems for online shopping or streaming services. By analyzing the graph structure, these systems can provide personalized recommendations to users.

Data visualization: Graphs are used to visualize and analyze complex data, such as in data mining and machine learning. By representing the data as a graph, we can better understand its structure and relationships.

Compiler design: Graphs are used to represent the control flow and data flow of programs, such as in optimizing compilers. By analyzing the graph structure, we can optimize the performance of the program and reduce its memory footprint.

In summary, graphs are a fundamental data structure in computer science with many applications in network analysis, pathfinding, recommendation systems, data visualization, and compiler design. By modeling real-world systems as graphs and analyzing their structure, we can gain insights into their behavior and optimize their performance.

2.11 What are the main types of sorting algorithms, and how do they differ in terms of performance?

Sorting algorithms are used to sort a list of elements in a specific order, such as ascending or descending. There are many different types of sorting algorithms, but the main ones are:

Bubble Sort: Bubble sort is a simple sorting algorithm that repeatedly steps through the list, compares adjacent elements and swaps them if they are in the wrong order. It has a worst-case time complexity of $O(n^2)$and is not efficient for large datasets.

Selection Sort: Selection sort is an in-place comparison sorting algorithm that divides the input list into two parts: the sublist of items already sorted, which is built up from left to right, and the sublist of items remaining to be sorted that occupy the rest of the list. It has a worst-case time complexity of $O(n^2)$ and is not efficient for large datasets.

Insertion Sort: Insertion sort is a simple sorting algorithm that builds the final sorted array one item at a time. It is much less efficient on large lists than more advanced algorithms such as quicksort, heapsort, or merge sort. It has a worst-case time complexity of $O(n^2)$ and is not efficient for large datasets.

Quick Sort: Quick sort is a divide-and-conquer sorting algorithm that works by selecting a 'pivot' element from the array and partitioning the other elements into two sub-arrays, according to whether they are less than or greater than the pivot. It has a worst-case time complexity of $O(n^2)$, but its average-case time complexity is O(n log n), making it efficient for large datasets.

Merge Sort: Merge sort is a divide-and-conquer sorting algorithm that divides the array into two halves, sorts each half separately, and then merges them back together. It has a worst-case time complexity of O(n log n), making it efficient for large datasets.

Heap Sort: Heap sort is a comparison-based sorting algorithm that builds a binary heap from the input array and then repeatedly extracts the maximum element and rebuilds the heap until the input array is sorted. It has a worst-case time complexity of O(n log n), making it efficient for large datasets.

In summary, the main types of sorting algorithms include bubble sort, selection sort, insertion sort, quick sort, merge sort, and heap sort. These algorithms differ in terms of their performance, with some being more efficient for large datasets than others. It is important to consider the dataset size and characteristics when choosing a sorting algorithm for a particular task.

2.12 Explain the difference between a singly-linked list and a doubly-linked list.

Both singly-linked lists and doubly-linked lists are linear data structures that store a collection of elements. However, the key difference between them is the number of links between each node and its neighboring nodes.

A singly-linked list is a linear data structure in which each node contains a value and a single link pointing to the next node in the list. The last node in the list has a link pointing to null, indicating the end of the list. Here is an example of a singly-linked list:

```
class Node {
    int value;
    Node next;

    public Node(int value) {
        this.value = value;
        this.next = null;
    }
}

class SinglyLinkedList {
    Node head;

    public SinglyLinkedList() {
        this.head = null;
    }

    public void add(int value) {
        Node newNode = new Node(value);
        if (head == null) {
            head = newNode;
        } else {
            Node current = head;
            while (current.next != null) {
                current = current.next;
            }
            current.next = newNode;
        }
    }
}
```

In this example, the Node class represents a node in the singly-linked list, with an integer value and a single link pointing to the next node in the list. The SinglyLinkedList class represents the singly-linked list itself, with a head node and a method for adding nodes to the end of the list.

A doubly-linked list, on the other hand, is a linear data structure in which each node contains a value and two links, one pointing to the previous node and one pointing to the next node in the list. The first node in the list has a link pointing to null for the previous node, and the last node in the list has a link pointing to null for the next node. Here is an example of a doubly-linked list:

```
class Node {
    int value;
    Node prev;
    Node next;

    public Node(int value) {
```

```
            this.value = value;
            this.prev = null;
            this.next = null;
        }
}

class DoublyLinkedList {
    Node head;
    Node tail;

    public DoublyLinkedList() {
        this.head = null;
        this.tail = null;
    }

    public void add(int value) {
        Node newNode = new Node(value);
        if (head == null) {
            head = newNode;
            tail = newNode;
        } else {
            newNode.prev = tail;
            tail.next = newNode;
            tail = newNode;
        }
    }
}
```

In this example, the Node class represents a node in the doubly-linked list, with an integer value and two links pointing to the previous node and the next node in the list. The DoublyLinkedList class represents the doubly-linked list itself, with a head node, a tail node, and a method for adding nodes to the end of the list.

In summary, the main difference between a singly-linked list and a doubly-linked list is that a singly-linked list has a single link pointing to the next node, while a doubly-linked list has two links pointing to the previous node and the next node. A doubly-linked list provides more flexibility in terms of traversing the list in both forward and backward directions, but requires more memory to store the extra links.

2.13 What is the time complexity of a linear search algorithm?

The time complexity of a linear search algorithm is $O(n)$, where n is the number of elements in the list or array being searched. This means that the worst-case time complexity of a linear search algorithm grows linearly with the size of the input.

In a linear search algorithm, we start at the first element of the list or array and compare it with the target value we are searching for. If the value matches, we return its index. If not, we move on to the next element and repeat the process until we find the target value or reach the end of the list or array.

Here is an example of a linear search algorithm in Java:

```java
public static int linearSearch(int[] arr, int target) {
    for (int i = 0; i < arr.length; i++) {
        if (arr[i] == target) {
            return i;
        }
    }
    return -1;
}
```

In this example, we pass in an integer array arr and a target value target. The algorithm iterates through each element of the array and checks if it matches the target value. If a match is found, the index of the element is returned. If no match is found, the function returns -1.

The worst-case time complexity of this algorithm is O(n), because in the worst case scenario, we will need to iterate through all n elements of the array before finding the target value or determining that it does not exist in the array.

In summary, the time complexity of a linear search algorithm is O(n), which means that its worst-case time complexity grows linearly with the size of the input. This algorithm is not efficient for large datasets, but it is simple and easy to implement for small datasets or when the elements are unsorted.

2.14 Describe the process of dynamic programming and provide an example.

Dynamic programming is an optimization technique used to solve complex problems by breaking them down into smaller, simpler subproblems and storing their solutions in a table for reuse. The main idea behind dynamic programming is to avoid recomputing solutions for the same subproblems, which can significantly improve the efficiency of the algorithm.

The dynamic programming approach involves the following steps:

Identify the subproblems: Break down the problem into smaller subproblems that can be solved independently. These subproblems should be related to each other and have overlapping substructures.

Define the state: Define the state for each subproblem, which includes all the necessary information to solve that subproblem. The state should be well-defined and consistent.

Formulate the recurrence relation: Express the solution to each subproblem in terms of its smaller subproblems. This recurrence relation should be recursive and include a base case for the smallest subproblems.

Solve the subproblems: Use the recurrence relation to solve each subproblem in a bottom-up or top-down manner, depending on the problem structure.

Store the solutions: Store the solutions to each subproblem in a table for reuse in solving other subproblems. This can significantly reduce the number of computations required and improve the overall efficiency of the algorithm.

Here is an example of dynamic programming: the Fibonacci sequence. The Fibonacci sequence is a sequence of numbers in which each number is the sum of the two preceding ones, starting from 0 and 1. The first few terms of the sequence are: 0, 1, 1, 2, 3, 5, 8, 13, 21, 34, 55, ...

The naive recursive implementation of the Fibonacci sequence has a time complexity of $O(2^n)$, which can quickly become computationally expensive for large values of n. However, using dynamic programming, we can solve the problem much more efficiently by storing the solutions to smaller subproblems in a table.

```
public static int fibonacci(int n) {
    if (n <= 1) {
        return n;
    }
    int[] table = new int[n+1];
    table[0] = 0;
    table[1] = 1;
```

```
    for (int i = 2; i <= n; i++) {
        table[i] = table[i-1] + table[i-2];
    }
    return table[n];
}
```

In this example, we use dynamic programming to calculate the nth term of the Fibonacci sequence. We first check if n is less than or equal to 1, in which case we return n. Otherwise, we create a table of size n+1 and initialize the first two values of the table to 0 and 1, respectively. We then use a for loop to iterate from 2 to n and calculate the value of each term in the Fibonacci sequence using the recurrence relation: table[i] = table[i-1] + table[i-2]. Finally, we return the value of the nth term in the sequence, which is stored in the last element of the table.

By using dynamic programming to solve the Fibonacci sequence, we reduce the time complexity from $O(2^n)$ to $O(n)$, which is much more efficient for large values of n. This is achieved by storing the solutions to smaller subproblems in the table and reusing them to solve larger subproblems, thus avoiding redundant computations.

2.15 What is a trie data structure, and what are its applications?

A trie (pronounced "try") is a tree-like data structure that is used for efficient retrieval of keys from a large set of strings or sequences. A trie is typically used to store a dictionary of words or sequences, with each node in the trie representing a character in the sequence.

Each node in a trie has a value and one or more child nodes, where each child node represents the next character in the sequence. The root node represents an empty string, and the leaf nodes represent the complete words or sequences. Here is an example of a trie that stores the words "cat", "car", "can", "dog", "doll", and "door":

```
    root
    / \
   c   d
  /|\   \
 a r n   o
/  |      \
t  e       o
   |       |
```

r   r

In this example, the root node represents an empty string. The node "c" has three child nodes representing the characters "a", "r", and "n", which in turn have child nodes representing the remaining characters in the words "cat", "car", and "can". The node "d" has two child nodes representing the characters "o" and "e", which in turn have child nodes representing the remaining characters in the words "dog", "doll", and "door".

The main advantage of a trie is that it provides fast lookup times for keys. The time complexity for searching a trie is $O(m)$, where m is the length of the key being searched. This is because each node in the trie corresponds to a character in the key, and we can traverse the trie by following the path corresponding to the characters in the key. If the key exists in the trie, we can reach the corresponding leaf node in $O(m)$ time.

Tries have many applications in computer science, including:

Autocomplete: Tries are commonly used in autocomplete features for text editors, search engines, and web browsers. As the user types, the trie is searched for the prefixes that match the current input, and a list of suggestions is generated based on the words or sequences that follow the prefixes.

Spell checking: Tries can be used to efficiently check the spelling of words in a document or input field. By storing a dictionary of words in a trie, we can quickly check if a given word is valid or not by traversing the trie and checking if the corresponding leaf node exists.

DNA sequencing: Tries can be used to store and search for DNA sequences in bioinformatics applications. By representing each nucleotide as a character in the trie, we can efficiently search for patterns and identify mutations in DNA sequences.

In summary, a trie is a tree-like data structure that is used for efficient retrieval of keys from a large set of strings or sequences. Tries provide fast lookup times for keys and have many applications in computer science, including autocomplete, spell checking, and DNA sequencing.

2.16   What is the difference between a binary search tree (BST) and a balanced binary search tree (such as an AVL tree)?

A binary search tree (BST) is a tree-based data structure in which each node has at most two children and the value of each node is greater than or equal to the values in its left subtree and less than or equal to the values in its right subtree. This ordering property allows for efficient search, insertion, and deletion operations in O(log n) time on average, where n is the number of nodes in the tree. However, if the tree is not balanced, the worst-case time complexity for these operations can be O(n), which is much less efficient.

A balanced binary search tree, such as an AVL tree, is a binary search tree that is automatically balanced to ensure that the height of the tree is always logarithmic in the number of nodes. This balance is achieved by performing rotations on the tree whenever a node is inserted or deleted that violates the ordering property or unbalances the tree.

The main difference between a binary search tree and a balanced binary search tree is in their performance. While both structures allow for efficient search, insertion, and deletion operations, the performance of a binary search tree can degrade significantly if the tree becomes unbalanced, leading to worst-case time complexity of O(n). On the other hand, a balanced binary search tree maintains a logarithmic height at all times, ensuring efficient operations in O(log n) time on average.

Here is an example of a binary search tree and a balanced binary search tree:

Binary search tree:

Balanced binary search tree (AVL tree):

In this example, both trees have the same structure and ordering property. However, the binary search tree is not balanced, as the left subtree has a height of 2 while the right subtree has a height of 1. This imbalance can lead to inefficiencies in search, insertion, and deletion operations, especially for large trees. The balanced binary search tree, on the other hand, is automatically balanced to ensure that the height of the tree is always logarithmic in the number of nodes, leading to more efficient operations.

In summary, a binary search tree and a balanced binary search tree differ in their performance and ability to maintain a logarithmic height. While a binary search tree can offer efficient operations on average, it can become inefficient if the tree becomes unbalanced. A balanced binary search tree, such as an AVL tree, maintains a logarithmic height at all times, ensuring efficient operations in O(log n) time on average.

2.17 What is the time complexity of the quicksort algorithm, and what is its worst-case scenario?

The quicksort algorithm is a widely used sorting algorithm that uses a divide-and-conquer approach to sort an array of elements in O(n log n) time on average, where n is the number of elements in the array. The algorithm works by selecting a pivot element from the array and partitioning the array into two subarrays, one containing elements less than or equal to the pivot, and one containing elements greater than the pivot. The algorithm then recursively sorts the two subarrays.

The time complexity of quicksort is O(n log n) on average, making it one of the fastest sorting algorithms for large datasets. This is because the algorithm's performance is dependent on the size of the subarrays being sorted, rather than the total number of elements in the array. In other words, the algorithm's time complexity grows logarithmically with the size of the subarrays.

However, the worst-case scenario for quicksort occurs when the pivot element is consistently chosen to be the minimum or maximum element in the array, resulting in unbalanced partitioning of the subarrays. In this case, the time complexity of the algorithm becomes $O(n^2)$, which is much less efficient than the average case. The worst-case scenario can be avoided by using a randomized pivot selection method or by selecting the pivot element from a median-of-three sample.

Here is an example of quicksort implementation in Java:

```java
public static void quicksort(int[] arr, int low, int high) {
    if (low < high) {
        int pivot = partition(arr, low, high);
        quicksort(arr, low, pivot-1);
        quicksort(arr, pivot+1, high);
    }
}

private static int partition(int[] arr, int low, int high) {
    int pivot = arr[high];
    int i = low - 1;
    for (int j = low; j < high; j++) {
        if (arr[j] < pivot) {
            i++;
            swap(arr, i, j);
        }
    }
    swap(arr, i+1, high);
    return i+1;
}

private static void swap(int[] arr, int i, int j) {
    int temp = arr[i];
    arr[i] = arr[j];
    arr[j] = temp;
}
```

In this example, we implement the quicksort algorithm in Java using a recursive approach. The quicksort function takes in an integer array arr, a lower index low, and an upper index high. If the lower index is less than the upper index, the function selects a pivot element using the partition function and recursively sorts the subarrays to the left and right of the pivot.

The partition function takes in the same inputs as quicksort and partitions the array into two subarrays by selecting the pivot element and rearranging the elements such that all elements less than the pivot are to the left of it and all elements greater than the pivot are to the right of it.

Overall, the quicksort algorithm has an average time complexity of $O(n \log n)$ and a worst-case time complexity of $O(n^2)$ when the pivot selection leads to unbalanced partitioning.

2.18 Explain the divide and conquer approach in algorithms. Provide an example where this technique is used.

The divide and conquer approach is a problem-solving technique used in algorithms that involves breaking a problem down into smaller subproblems, solving each subproblem independently, and then combining the solutions of the subproblems to solve the original problem. This approach is particularly useful for solving complex problems that are difficult to solve directly, as it allows us to break down the problem into smaller, more manageable pieces.

The divide and conquer approach typically involves three steps:

Divide: Break the problem down into smaller subproblems that can be solved independently. Conquer: Solve each subproblem independently using the same approach. Combine: Combine the solutions of the subproblems to solve the original problem.

An example of a problem that can be solved using the divide and conquer approach is the merge sort algorithm, which is a sorting algorithm that uses the divide and conquer approach to sort an array of elements in $O(n \log n)$ time.

The merge sort algorithm works by dividing the input array into two halves, recursively sorting each half using the same approach, and then merging the sorted halves back together to create a fully sorted array. Here is an example implementation of the merge sort algorithm in Java:

```java
public static void mergeSort(int[] arr, int left, int right) {
    if (left < right) {
        int mid = (left + right) / 2;
```

```
        mergeSort(arr, left, mid);
        mergeSort(arr, mid+1, right);
        merge(arr, left, mid, right);
    }
}

private static void merge(int[] arr, int left, int mid, int right) {
    int[] temp = new int[right - left + 1];
    int i = left, j = mid+1, k = 0;
    while (i <= mid && j <= right) {
        if (arr[i] < arr[j]) {
            temp[k++] = arr[i++];
        } else {
            temp[k++] = arr[j++];
        }
    }
    while (i <= mid) {
        temp[k++] = arr[i++];
    }
    while (j <= right) {
        temp[k++] = arr[j++];
    }
    for (i = left; i <= right; i++) {
        arr[i] = temp[i - left];
    }
}
```

In this example, the mergeSort function takes in an integer array arr, a left index left, and a right index right. If the left index is less than the right index, the function selects a midpoint using integer division and recursively sorts the left and right halves of the array using the mergeSort function. Once the two halves are sorted, the merge function is called to combine the two sorted halves into a fully sorted array.

The merge function takes in the same inputs as mergeSort and merges the left and right halves of the array into a single sorted array by comparing the elements in each half and adding them to a temporary array in sorted order.

Overall, the merge sort algorithm is an example of the divide and conquer approach in algorithms, as it breaks down the sorting problem into smaller subproblems, sorts each subproblem independently, and then combines the solutions to create a fully sorted array.

2.19 What are the differences between in-order, pre-order, and post-order tree traversals? Provide a brief description of each traversal method.

In-order, pre-order, and post-order are different traversal methods used to visit the nodes of a binary tree. Each traversal method visits the nodes in a different order, resulting in different outputs and different use cases.

In-order traversal: In an in-order traversal, the left subtree is visited first, followed by the root node, and then the right subtree. This traversal method is commonly used to visit the nodes of a binary search tree in sorted order, as it visits the nodes in ascending order of their values.

Here is an example of in-order traversal in Java:

```java
public static void inOrderTraversal(Node root) {
    if (root != null) {
        inOrderTraversal(root.left);
        System.out.print(root.val + " ");
        inOrderTraversal(root.right);
    }
}
```

Pre-order traversal: In a pre-order traversal, the root node is visited first, followed by the left subtree, and then the right subtree. This traversal method is commonly used to create a copy of the binary tree, as it visits the nodes in the order in which they would be copied.

Here is an example of pre-order traversal in Java:

```java
public static void preOrderTraversal(Node root) {
    if (root != null) {
        System.out.print(root.val + " ");
        preOrderTraversal(root.left);
        preOrderTraversal(root.right);
    }
}
```

Post-order traversal: In a post-order traversal, the left subtree is visited first, followed by the right subtree, and then the root node. This traversal method is commonly used to delete the binary tree, as it visits the nodes in the order in which they would be deleted.

Here is an example of post-order traversal in Java:

```java
public static void postOrderTraversal(Node root) {
    if (root != null) {
        postOrderTraversal(root.left);
        postOrderTraversal(root.right);
        System.out.print(root.val + " ");
    }
}
```

Overall, the differences between in-order, pre-order, and post-order tree traversals lie in the order in which the nodes are visited. While in-order traversal visits the left subtree first, pre-order traversal visits the root node first, and post-order traversal visits the root node last. These traversal methods can be used for different purposes, such as visiting the nodes in sorted order, creating a copy of the binary tree, or deleting the binary tree.

2.20 What is a priority queue, and how is it implemented using a heap data structure?

A priority queue is a data structure that stores a collection of elements, each with a priority, and allows elements with higher priorities to be dequeued or removed before elements with lower priorities. Priority queues are commonly used in algorithms such as Dijkstra's shortest path algorithm and Huffman coding.

One way to implement a priority queue is using a heap data structure, which is a complete binary tree where each node has a priority value that is either greater than or equal to its children's priority values (in a max heap) or less than or equal to its children's priority values (in a min heap).

In a max heap implementation of a priority queue, the element with the highest priority (i.e., the largest priority value) is stored at the root of the heap, and elements are dequeued by removing the root and reorganizing the heap so that the next highest priority element becomes the new root.

Here is an example implementation of a max heap-based priority queue in Java:

```
public class PriorityQueue {
    private int[] heap;
    private int size;

    public PriorityQueue(int capacity) {
        heap = new int[capacity];
        size = 0;
    }

    public boolean isEmpty() {
        return size == 0;
    }

    public boolean isFull() {
        return size == heap.length;
    }

    public void enqueue(int value) {
        if (isFull()) {
            throw new IllegalStateException("Priority queue is full.
                ");
        }
        heap[size] = value;
        siftUp(size);
        size++;
    }

    public int dequeue() {
        if (isEmpty()) {
            throw new IllegalStateException("Priority queue is empty
                .");
        }
        int result = heap[0];
        size--;
        heap[0] = heap[size];
        siftDown(0);
        return result;
    }

    private void siftUp(int index) {
        int parentIndex = (index - 1) / 2;
        if (index > 0 && heap[index] > heap[parentIndex]) {
            swap(index, parentIndex);
            siftUp(parentIndex);
        }
    }

    private void siftDown(int index) {
        int leftChildIndex = 2 * index + 1;
        int rightChildIndex = 2 * index + 2;
        int maxIndex = index;
        if (leftChildIndex < size && heap[leftChildIndex] > heap[
            maxIndex]) {
            maxIndex = leftChildIndex;
        }
        if (rightChildIndex < size && heap[rightChildIndex] > heap[
            maxIndex]) {
            maxIndex = rightChildIndex;
        }
        if (index != maxIndex) {
            swap(index, maxIndex);
            siftDown(maxIndex);
```

```
        }
    }

    private void swap(int i, int j) {
        int temp = heap[i];
        heap[i] = heap[j];
        heap[j] = temp;
    }
}
```

In this implementation, the priority queue is represented using a max heap data structure stored in an integer array called heap. The size variable keeps track of the number of elements in the priority queue.

The enqueue method inserts a new element into the priority queue and ensures that the heap property is maintained by calling the siftUp method, which swaps the new element with its parent if it has a higher priority.

The dequeue method removes the element with the highest priority from the priority queue and ensures that the heap property is maintained by calling the siftDown method, which swaps the root element with its highest priority child until the heap property is restored.

The siftUp method compares the priority of the new element with its parent's priority and swaps them if necessary to maintain the heap property.

Chapter 3

Intermediate

3.1 What is the concept of time complexity and space complexity? How do they impact algorithm efficiency?

Time complexity and space complexity are two important concepts used to analyze the efficiency of algorithms.

Time complexity refers to the amount of time it takes for an algorithm to run as a function of its input size. It measures how the runtime of the algorithm grows with the size of the input, and is typically expressed using big O notation. For example, an algorithm with a time complexity of O(n) has a linear runtime, meaning that its runtime increases linearly with the size of the input. An algorithm with a time complexity of $O(n^2)$ has a quadratic runtime, meaning that its runtime increases quadratically with the size of the input.

Space complexity refers to the amount of memory an algorithm uses as a function of its input size. It measures how much memory the algorithm requires to run, and is typically expressed using big O notation as well. For example, an algorithm with a space complexity of O(1) uses a constant amount of memory, meaning that its memory usage does not depend on the size of the input. An algorithm with a space complexity of O(n) uses a linear amount of memory, meaning that its memory usage grows linearly with the size of the input.

The time and space complexity of an algorithm are important factors in determining its efficiency. Algorithms with better time and space complexity are generally considered more efficient, as they can handle larger inputs and run faster than less efficient algorithms. However, optimizing for one factor may come at the cost of the other. For example, an algorithm that uses more memory may run faster than an algorithm with a lower space complexity, but may not be suitable for systems with limited memory.

It is important for programmers to consider both time and space complexity when designing and implementing algorithms, and to choose the appropriate algorithm for the problem at hand based on the requirements for time and space efficiency.

3.2 Explain the difference between the best-case, average-case, and worst-case time complexities of an algorithm.

The best-case, average-case, and worst-case time complexities of an algorithm are measures of how efficient the algorithm is under different scenarios of input.

The best-case time complexity refers to the minimum amount of time an algorithm can take to complete its execution. This occurs when the input is already sorted, or when the algorithm can take advantage of some special property of the input to finish its execution quickly. The best-case time complexity of an algorithm is typically denoted by the big omega notation (), and it represents the lower bound of the algorithm's runtime.

For example, the best-case time complexity of a linear search algorithm is O(1), which occurs when the target element is the first element of the array.

The worst-case time complexity refers to the maximum amount of time an algorithm can take to complete its execution. This occurs when the input is arranged in a way that makes the algorithm perform the maximum number of operations. The worst-case time complexity of an algorithm is typically denoted by the big O notation (O), and it represents the upper bound of the algorithm's runtime.

For example, the worst-case time complexity of a linear search algorithm is $O(n)$, which occurs when the target element is not present in the array, and the algorithm has to traverse the entire array.

The average-case time complexity refers to the expected amount of time an algorithm takes to complete its execution when the input is drawn from a probability distribution. The average-case time complexity is typically denoted by the big theta notation (), and it represents the average or typical runtime of the algorithm for a given input distribution.

For example, the average-case time complexity of a quicksort algorithm is $O(n \log n)$, which occurs when the input is drawn from a uniform distribution.

In summary, the best-case time complexity represents the lower bound of an algorithm's runtime, the worst-case time complexity represents the upper bound, and the average-case time complexity represents the expected runtime under a given input distribution. The choice of which time complexity to optimize for depends on the specific requirements of the problem at hand.

3.3 Can you describe the merge sort algorithm and its time complexity?

Merge sort is a sorting algorithm that follows the divide-and-conquer paradigm. It works by recursively dividing the input array into smaller sub-arrays, sorting them, and then merging them back together to produce a sorted output array.

The merge sort algorithm can be summarized as follows:

- Divide the unsorted array into n sub-arrays, each containing one element.

- Repeat the following steps until there is only one sorted sub-array remaining:

- a. Divide each sub-array into two sub-arrays of roughly equal size.

- b. Sort the two sub-arrays recursively by repeating step 2.

- c. Merge the two sorted sub-arrays into a single sorted sub-array by comparing the elements in each sub-array and inserting them into a new array in sorted order.

- The single sorted sub-array is the final sorted array.

Here is an example implementation of the merge sort algorithm in Java:

```java
public static void mergeSort(int[] arr) {
    if (arr.length > 1) {
        int mid = arr.length / 2;
        int[] left = Arrays.copyOfRange(arr, 0, mid);
        int[] right = Arrays.copyOfRange(arr, mid, arr.length);
        mergeSort(left);
        mergeSort(right);
        merge(arr, left, right);
    }
}

public static void merge(int[] arr, int[] left, int[] right) {
    int i = 0, j = 0, k = 0;
    while (i < left.length && j < right.length) {
        if (left[i] < right[j]) {
            arr[k++] = left[i++];
        } else {
            arr[k++] = right[j++];
        }
    }
    while (i < left.length) {
        arr[k++] = left[i++];
    }
    while (j < right.length) {
        arr[k++] = right[j++];
    }
}
```

In this implementation, the mergeSort method takes an integer array as input and sorts it using the merge sort algorithm. If the length of the array is greater than 1, it splits the array into two sub-arrays and sorts them recursively using the mergeSort method. It then merges the two sorted sub-arrays using the merge method.

The merge method takes three integer arrays as input: the original array arr and the two sorted sub-arrays left and right. It compares the elements in the two sub-arrays and inserts them into the original array in sorted order.

The time complexity of the merge sort algorithm is O(n log n) in the worst case, where n is the size of the input array. This is because the algorithm divides the input array into two sub-arrays of roughly equal size log n times, and then merges them back together in linear time n times. The merge operation takes O(n) time in the worst case, and it is performed log n times, leading to an overall time complexity of O(n log n).

3.4 How does the insertion sort algorithm work, and what is its time complexity?

Insertion sort is a simple sorting algorithm that works by iterating over the input array and repeatedly inserting each element into its correct position in a sorted portion of the array. The sorted portion of the array starts with the first element and grows by one element each iteration until the entire array is sorted.

The insertion sort algorithm can be summarized as follows:

Iterate over the unsorted array from the second element to the last element. For each element, compare it to the elements in the sorted portion of the array from right to left until the correct position is found. Insert the element into its correct position in the sorted portion of the array by shifting the elements to the right. Repeat steps 2-3 for the remaining unsorted elements.

Here is an example implementation of the insertion sort algorithm in Java:

```java
public static void insertionSort(int[] arr) {
    for (int i = 1; i < arr.length; i++) {
        int key = arr[i];
        int j = i - 1;
        while (j >= 0 && arr[j] > key) {
            arr[j + 1] = arr[j];
            j--;
        }
```

```
        arr[j + 1] = key;
    }
}
```

In this implementation, the insertionSort method takes an integer array as input and sorts it using the insertion sort algorithm. It iterates over the array from the second element to the last element, and for each element, it compares it to the elements in the sorted portion of the array from right to left until the correct position is found. It then inserts the element into its correct position by shifting the elements to the right.

The time complexity of the insertion sort algorithm is $O(n^2)$ in the worst case, where n is the size of the input array. This is because the algorithm performs one comparison and one shift operation for each element in the array, leading to a nested loop structure and a time complexity of $O(n^2)$. However, the best case time complexity is $O(n)$ when the array is already sorted, and the average case time complexity is also $O(n^2)$, making it less efficient than other sorting algorithms such as quicksort and mergesort for large input sizes.

3.5 What are the primary operations of a stack, and how do they work?

A stack is a data structure that allows elements to be added and removed in a last-in, first-out (LIFO) order. The primary operations of a stack are push and pop.

The push operation adds an element to the top of the stack. It takes a single argument, the element to be added, and adds it to the top of the stack. The new element becomes the top element of the stack, and all other elements are shifted down by one position. For example, consider the following implementation of a stack using an array in Java:

```java
public class Stack {
    private int[] data;
    private int top;

    public Stack(int capacity) {
        data = new int[capacity];
        top = -1;
    }
```

```
public void push(int element) {
    if (top == data.length - 1) {
        throw new IllegalStateException("Stack overflow");
    }
    top++;
    data[top] = element;
    }
}
```

In this implementation, the push method takes an integer argument element and adds it to the top of the stack. It first checks if the stack is full by comparing the top index to the length of the array, and throws an exception if the stack is full. Otherwise, it increments the top index and sets the value of the new top element to element.

The pop operation removes the top element from the stack. It takes no arguments, and returns the element that was removed. The top element of the stack is removed, and the element immediately below it becomes the new top element. For example, consider the following implementation of a stack using an array in Java:

```
public class Stack {
    private int[] data;
    private int top;

    public Stack(int capacity) {
        data = new int[capacity];
        top = -1;
    }

    public int pop() {
        if (top == -1) {
            throw new NoSuchElementException("Stack underflow");
        }
        int element = data[top];
        top--;
        return element;
    }
}
```

In this implementation, the pop method removes the top element from the stack and returns it. It first checks if the stack is empty by comparing the top index to -1, and throws an exception if the stack is empty. Otherwise, it retrieves the value of the top element and decrements the top index.

Other operations that may be supported by a stack include peek, which retrieves the top element without removing it, and isEmpty, which checks if the stack is empty. These operations are commonly used in conjunction with the push and pop operations to manipulate the elements in the stack.

3.6 Describe the primary operations of a queue, and explain how a circular queue can be implemented.

A queue is a data structure that allows elements to be added at the rear and removed from the front in a first-in, first-out (FIFO) order. The primary operations of a queue are enqueue and dequeue.

The enqueue operation adds an element to the rear of the queue. It takes a single argument, the element to be added, and adds it to the end of the queue. For example, consider the following implementation of a queue using an array in Java:

```java
public class Queue {
    private int[] data;
    private int front, rear;

    public Queue(int capacity) {
        data = new int[capacity];
        front = -1;
        rear = -1;
    }

    public void enqueue(int element) {
        if (rear == data.length - 1) {
            throw new IllegalStateException("Queue␣overflow");
        }
        rear++;
        data[rear] = element;
        if (front == -1) {
            front = 0;
        }
    }
}
```

In this implementation, the enqueue method takes an integer argument element and adds it to the rear of the queue. It first checks if the queue is full by comparing the rear index to the length of the array, and throws an exception if the queue is full. Otherwise, it increments the rear index and sets the value of the new rear element to element. If this is the first element to be added to the queue, it sets the front index to 0.

The dequeue operation removes the element at the front of the queue. It takes no arguments, and returns the element that was removed. The front element of the queue is removed, and the element immediately behind it becomes the new front element. For example, consider the following implementation of a queue using an array in Java:

```
public class Queue {
    private int[] data;
    private int front, rear;

    public Queue(int capacity) {
        data = new int[capacity];
        front = -1;
        rear = -1;
    }

    public int dequeue() {
        if (front == -1 || front > rear) {
            throw new NoSuchElementException("Queue underflow");
        }
        int element = data[front];
        front++;
        return element;
    }
}
```

In this implementation, the dequeue method removes the front element from the queue and returns it. It first checks if the queue is empty by comparing the front index to -1, or if the front index is greater than the rear index, and throws an exception if the queue is empty. Otherwise, it retrieves the value of the front element and increments the front index.

A circular queue is a variation of the queue data structure in which the rear and front indices are connected, allowing the queue to wrap around to the beginning of the array when it reaches the end. This allows the queue to reuse the space at the beginning of the array once the elements at the front of the queue have been dequeued, and can be useful in cases where the size of the queue is fixed and a dynamic resizing operation is not desirable.

Here is an example implementation of a circular queue using an array in Java:

```
public class CircularQueue {
    private int[] data;
    private int front, rear, size;

    public CircularQueue(int capacity) {
        data = new int[capacity];
        front = 0;
```

```
        rear = -1;
        size = 0;
}

public void enqueue(int element) {
    if (size == data.length) {
        throw new IllegalStateException("Queue␣overflow");
    }
    rear = (rear + 1) % data.length;
    data[rear] = element;
    size++;
}
```

3.7 What is a directed and undirected graph? Provide examples of each type.

A graph is a data structure that consists of a set of vertices (nodes) and a set of edges that connect pairs of vertices. A directed graph, also known as a digraph, is a graph in which each edge has a direction, indicating that the edge connects one vertex to another in a specific direction. An undirected graph is a graph in which each edge has no direction, indicating that the edge connects two vertices without a specific direction.

Here are examples of directed and undirected graphs:

Directed graph: A social media platform that models friendships between users as directed edges. If user A is friends with user B, there is a directed edge from A to B. This graph is directed because the relationship between users is not necessarily mutual - user A can be friends with user B without user B being friends with user A.

Undirected graph: A map that models the connections between cities as edges. If there is a road that connects city A to city B, there is an undirected edge between A and B. This graph is undirected because the connection between cities is bidirectional - if there is a road from A to B, there is also a road from B to A.

In general, directed graphs are useful for modeling relationships that have a specific direction, such as the flow of traffic on a road network or the dependencies between tasks in a project. Undirected graphs are useful for modeling relationships that are bidirectional, such as the connections between nodes in a computer network or the relationships between items in a recommendation system.

3.8 Explain the difference between weighted and unweighted graphs.

The difference between weighted and unweighted graphs lies in the values associated with their edges.

In an unweighted graph, all edges have the same value or weight, which is typically 1. This means that there is no distinction between different edges, and the shortest path between two vertices is the path with the fewest number of edges. For example, consider a graph representing a road network between cities, where each city is a vertex and each edge represents a road connecting two cities. In an unweighted graph, each road has the same weight, so the shortest path between two cities is the path with the fewest number of roads.

In a weighted graph, each edge has a value or weight associated with it, which can represent a variety of quantities such as distance, cost, or time. This means that some edges may be more important than others, and the shortest path between two vertices is not necessarily the path with the fewest number of edges. For example, consider a graph representing a flight network between cities, where each city is a vertex and each edge represents a flight between two cities. In a weighted graph, each flight has a different duration or cost, so the shortest path between two cities may involve taking a longer flight with a lower cost or a shorter flight with a higher cost.

Weighted graphs are useful for modeling real-world scenarios where the edges have varying degrees of importance or cost. They can be used in various applications such as route planning, resource allocation, and network optimization.

3.9   Can you describe Dijkstra's shortest path algorithm?

Dijkstra's shortest path algorithm is an algorithm used to find the shortest path between two vertices in a weighted graph. The algorithm works by maintaining a set of visited vertices and a set of unvisited vertices, and assigning a tentative distance to each vertex representing the shortest known distance from the source vertex to that vertex. The algorithm repeatedly selects the unvisited vertex with the smallest tentative distance, updates the distances of its neighboring vertices if a shorter path is found, and marks the vertex as visited. The algorithm continues until the destination vertex is marked as visited, or all vertices have been visited and there is no path from the source vertex to the destination vertex.

Here are the steps for Dijkstra's shortest path algorithm:

Create a set of unvisited vertices, and assign a tentative distance of infinity to all vertices except the source vertex, which is assigned a tentative distance of 0.

While there are unvisited vertices:

- a. Select the unvisited vertex with the smallest tentative distance.

- b. For each neighboring vertex, calculate the distance from the source vertex through the current vertex, and update the tentative distance if it is shorter than the current distance.

- c. Mark the current vertex as visited.

If the destination vertex has been marked as visited, terminate the algorithm. Otherwise, there is no path from the source vertex to the destination vertex.

The shortest path from the source vertex to the destination vertex can be found by tracing back from the destination vertex to the source vertex, following the path with the lowest cumulative weight.

Here is an example implementation of Dijkstra's shortest path algorithm in Java:

```java
public class Dijkstra {
    public static int[] shortestPath(int[][] graph, int source) {
        int n = graph.length;
        int[] distance = new int[n];
        boolean[] visited = new boolean[n];
        Arrays.fill(distance, Integer.MAX_VALUE);
        distance[source] = 0;

        for (int i = 0; i < n; i++) {
            int current = findMin(distance, visited);
            visited[current] = true;

            for (int j = 0; j < n; j++) {
                if (graph[current][j] != 0 && !visited[j]) {
                    int newDistance = distance[current] + graph[
                        current][j];
                    if (newDistance < distance[j]) {
                        distance[j] = newDistance;
                    }
                }
            }
        }
        return distance;
    }

    private static int findMin(int[] distance, boolean[] visited) {
        int min = Integer.MAX_VALUE;
        int index = -1;
        for (int i = 0; i < distance.length; i++) {
            if (distance[i] < min && !visited[i]) {
                min = distance[i];
                index = i;
            }
        }
        return index;
    }
}
```

In this implementation, the shortestPath method takes a two-dimensional array graph representing the weighted graph and an integer source representing the source vertex, and returns an array representing the shortest distance from the source vertex to each vertex in the graph. The findMin method is a helper method used to find the unvisited vertex with the smallest tentative distance. The algorithm initializes the distance array to infinity for all vertices except the source vertex, sets the source vertex as visited, and updates the tentative distances of its neighboring vertices. The algorithm continues to update the tentative distances and visit the unvisited vertex with the smallest tentative distance until all vertices have been visited or the destination vertex is marked as visited. Finally, the shortest path can be traced back from the destination vertex to the source vertex using the distance array.

3.10 What is the difference between a min-heap and a max-heap?

A heap is a data structure that can be visualized as a binary tree with two properties: the heap property and the shape property. The heap property specifies that for every node in the tree, its parent node is either smaller (in a min-heap) or larger (in a max-heap) than its child nodes. The shape property specifies that the tree is a complete binary tree, meaning that all levels of the tree are completely filled except possibly the last level, which is filled from left to right.

The difference between a min-heap and a max-heap is in the ordering of the nodes with respect to the heap property. In a min-heap, the value of the parent node is smaller than the value of its child nodes, while in a max-heap, the value of the parent node is larger than the value of its child nodes.

Here are some examples of min-heaps and max-heaps:

Min-heap:

```
2
/
3 5
/ \ /
8 9 7 6
```

Max-heap:

```
8
/
7 6
/ \ /
2 3 5 4
```

Min-heaps and max-heaps are useful for implementing priority queues, where the smallest (or largest) element is always at the top of the heap and can be efficiently accessed and removed. They are also used in various graph algorithms such as Dijkstra's shortest path algorithm and Prim's minimum spanning tree algorithm.

3.11 How can a binary search tree be used to implement a map or dictionary data structure?

A binary search tree (BST) is a data structure that stores elements in a binary tree, where each node has at most two children and satisfies the BST property: for each node, all nodes in its left subtree have keys less than the node's key, and all nodes in its right subtree have keys greater than the node's key. This property allows for efficient searching, insertion, and deletion of elements.

A map or dictionary is a data structure that stores key-value pairs and allows for efficient retrieval, insertion, and deletion of elements based on their keys. One way to implement a map or dictionary data structure is to use a binary search tree, where the keys are stored in the tree nodes and the values are stored as the values of the tree nodes.

Here is an example implementation of a BST-based map in Java:

```java
public class BSTMap<K extends Comparable<K>, V> {
    private Node root;

    private class Node {
        K key;
        V value;
        Node left;
        Node right;

        public Node(K key, V value) {
            this.key = key;
            this.value = value;
        }
    }

    public void put(K key, V value) {
        root = put(root, key, value);
    }

    private Node put(Node node, K key, V value) {
        if (node == null) {
            return new Node(key, value);
        }
        int cmp = key.compareTo(node.key);
        if (cmp < 0) {
            node.left = put(node.left, key, value);
        } else if (cmp > 0) {
            node.right = put(node.right, key, value);
        } else {
            node.value = value;
        }
        return node;
```

```
    }

    public V get(K key) {
        Node node = get(root, key);
        return node == null ? null : node.value;
    }

    private Node get(Node node, K key) {
        if (node == null) {
            return null;
        }
        int cmp = key.compareTo(node.key);
        if (cmp < 0) {
            return get(node.left, key);
        } else if (cmp > 0) {
            return get(node.right, key);
        } else {
            return node;
        }
    }

    public void delete(K key) {
        root = delete(root, key);
    }

    private Node delete(Node node, K key) {
        if (node == null) {
            return null;
        }
        int cmp = key.compareTo(node.key);
        if (cmp < 0) {
            node.left = delete(node.left, key);
        } else if (cmp > 0) {
            node.right = delete(node.right, key);
        } else {
            if (node.left == null) {
                return node.right;
            } else if (node.right == null) {
                return node.left;
            } else {
                Node min = min(node.right);
                min.right = deleteMin(node.right);
                min.left = node.left;
                node = min;
            }
        }
        return node;
    }

    private Node min(Node node) {
        if (node.left == null) {
            return node;
        }
        return min(node.left);
    }

    private Node deleteMin(Node node) {
        if (node.left == null) {
            return node.right;
        }
        node.left = deleteMin(node.left);
        return node;
```

```
    }
}
```

In this implementation, the BSTMap class uses a nested Node class to represent the nodes of the binary search tree. The put method inserts a key-value pair into the tree by recursively searching for the appropriate position to insert the node based on the key.

3.12 What is topological sorting, and in which situations is it useful?

Topological sorting is a technique used to order the vertices in a directed acyclic graph (DAG) in a way that preserves the ordering of the edges. In other words, if there is a directed edge from vertex A to vertex B in the graph, then A must come before B in the topological ordering.

Topological sorting can be done using depth-first search (DFS) or breadth-first search (BFS) algorithms. The basic idea is to visit each vertex in the graph and add it to the output list in reverse order of its finishing time. The finishing time of a vertex is the time at which all of its adjacent vertices have been visited and added to the output list.

Topological sorting is useful in situations where there is a dependency between tasks or events, and the tasks or events must be completed in a specific order to avoid conflicts or errors. For example, in a software build system, there may be a set of dependencies between the source code files, where one file must be compiled before another file can be compiled. By performing a topological sort of the dependency graph, the build system can ensure that the source code files are compiled in the correct order to produce a working program.

Here is an example of a topological sorting algorithm using DFS in Java:

```java
import java.util.*;

public class TopologicalSort {
    private boolean[] visited;
    private Stack<Integer> stack;
```

```
public List<Integer> topologicalSort(int numVertices, List<List<
    Integer>> adjList) {
    visited = new boolean[numVertices];
    stack = new Stack<>();
    for (int i = 0; i < numVertices; i++) {
        if (!visited[i]) {
            dfs(i, adjList);
        }
    }
    List<Integer> result = new ArrayList<>();
    while (!stack.isEmpty()) {
        result.add(stack.pop());
    }
    return result;
}

private void dfs(int vertex, List<List<Integer>> adjList) {
    visited[vertex] = true;
    for (int adjVertex : adjList.get(vertex)) {
        if (!visited[adjVertex]) {
            dfs(adjVertex, adjList);
        }
    }
    stack.push(vertex);
}
```

In this implementation, the topologicalSort method takes as input the number of vertices in the graph and an adjacency list representation of the graph. It initializes a boolean array to keep track of visited vertices and a stack to store the vertices in reverse order of their finishing times. It then performs a DFS traversal of the graph, visiting each unvisited vertex and recursively visiting its adjacent vertices. When the DFS traversal of a vertex is complete, it is added to the stack. Finally, the vertices are popped off the stack in reverse order to produce the topological sort.

3.13 Explain how the concept of memoization is used in dynamic programming.

Memoization is a technique used in dynamic programming to reduce the time complexity of an algorithm by caching the results of expensive function calls and reusing them when the same inputs occur again. It is a form of caching where the results of expensive computations are stored in memory and retrieved later when needed, rather than being recomputed every time the function is called with the same inputs.

Memoization is particularly useful in dynamic programming, where a problem is solved by breaking it down into smaller subproblems that are solved independently and combined to solve the larger problem. In these cases, memoization can help to avoid redundant computation by caching the solutions to the subproblems and reusing them later when needed.

Here is an example of a memoized Fibonacci function in Java:

```java
import java.util.*;

public class MemoizedFibonacci {
    private Map<Integer, Integer> cache = new HashMap<>();

    public int fibonacci(int n) {
        if (cache.containsKey(n)) {
            return cache.get(n);
        }
        int result;
        if (n == 0 || n == 1) {
            result = n;
        } else {
            result = fibonacci(n - 1) + fibonacci(n - 2);
        }
        cache.put(n, result);
        return result;
    }
}
```

In this implementation, the fibonacci method takes an integer n and computes the nth Fibonacci number recursively. Before computing the result, it checks whether the result is already present in the cache. If it is, it returns the cached result. If not, it computes the result recursively using the formula fibonacci(n) = fibonacci(n-1) + fibonacci(n-2) and stores the result in the cache for later use. By using memoization, the time complexity of the function is reduced from exponential to linear, since each value is computed only once and stored for later use.

3.14 Describe the Knapsack Problem and how dynamic programming can be used to solve it.

The Knapsack Problem is a classic optimization problem in computer science and operations research. It involves packing a knapsack with items of various weights and values, with the goal of maximizing the total value while keeping the weight within a certain limit.

Formally, the problem can be stated as follows: Given a set of items, each with a weight and a value, and a knapsack with a maximum weight capacity, determine the maximum value that can be obtained by packing the knapsack with a subset of the items.

Dynamic programming can be used to solve the Knapsack Problem by breaking it down into smaller subproblems and solving them independently. The basic idea is to construct a table that represents the optimal solution for all possible subproblems of the original problem, and then use this table to compute the optimal solution for the entire problem.

Here is an example implementation of the Knapsack Problem using dynamic programming in Java:

```java
public class Knapsack {
    public int knapsack(int[] weights, int[] values, int capacity) {
        int[][] table = new int[weights.length + 1][capacity + 1];
        for (int i = 1; i <= weights.length; i++) {
            for (int j = 1; j <= capacity; j++) {
                if (weights[i-1] > j) {
                    table[i][j] = table[i-1][j];
                } else {
                    table[i][j] = Math.max(table[i-1][j], table[i
                        -1][j-weights[i-1]] + values[i-1]);
                }
            }
        }
        return table[weights.length][capacity];
    }
}
```

In this implementation, the knapsack method takes as input an array of weights, an array of values, and a capacity. It initializes a table of size (weights.length + 1) x (capacity + 1) to store the optimal solutions to all possible subproblems. It then iterates through the table, computing the optimal solution for each subproblem based on the solutions to its smaller subproblems. The optimal solution for the entire problem is then found in the bottom-right corner of the table.

The time complexity of the Knapsack Problem using dynamic programming is $O(nW)$, where n is the number of items and W is the maximum weight capacity of the knapsack. This is significantly more efficient than the brute-force approach, which has a time complexity of $O(2^n)$.

3.15 What is the Longest Common Subsequence problem, and how can it be solved using dynamic programming?

The Longest Common Subsequence (LCS) problem is a classic computer science problem that involves finding the longest subsequence that is common to two given sequences. A subsequence is a sequence that can be derived from another sequence by deleting some elements without changing the order of the remaining elements. For example, the LCS of the sequences "ABCDGH" and "AEDFHR" is "ADH", with a length of 3.

Dynamic programming can be used to solve the LCS problem efficiently by breaking it down into smaller subproblems and solving them independently. The basic idea is to construct a table that represents the lengths of the LCSs for all possible pairs of prefixes of the two sequences, and then use this table to compute the length of the LCS for the entire sequences.

Here is an example implementation of the LCS problem using dynamic programming in Java:

```
public class LCS {
    public int lcs(char[] X, char[] Y, int m, int n) {
        int[][] table = new int[m+1][n+1];
        for (int i = 0; i <= m; i++) {
            for (int j = 0; j <= n; j++) {
                if (i == 0 || j == 0) {
                    table[i][j] = 0;
                } else if (X[i-1] == Y[j-1]) {
```

```
            table[i][j] = 1 + table[i-1][j-1];
        } else {
            table[i][j] = Math.max(table[i-1][j], table[i][j
                -1]);
        }
    }
}
return table[m][n];
}
}
```

In this implementation, the lcs method takes as input two character arrays X and Y, and their lengths m and n, respectively. It
initializes a table of size (m+1) x (n+1) to store the lengths of
the LCSs for all possible pairs of prefixes of X and Y. It then iterates through the table, computing the lengths of the LCSs for
each pair of prefixes based on the lengths of their smaller prefixes.
The length of the LCS for the entire sequences is then found in the
bottom-right corner of the table.

The time complexity of the LCS problem using dynamic programming is O(mn), where m and n are the lengths of the input sequences. This is significantly more efficient than the brute-force
approach, which has a time complexity of $O(2^n)$.

3.16   Can you explain the Bellman-Ford algorithm and its use cases?

The Bellman-Ford algorithm is a single-source shortest path algorithm that can be used to find the shortest path between a source
vertex and all other vertices in a weighted directed graph. It is
capable of handling negative edge weights, which makes it more
versatile than the Dijkstra's algorithm. However, its time complexity is higher than Dijkstra's algorithm.

The basic idea behind the Bellman-Ford algorithm is to relax all
edges in the graph repeatedly, starting from the source vertex, until
no further improvements can be made. The algorithm maintains
a distance array that stores the current shortest distance from the
source vertex to each vertex in the graph. Initially, all distances
are set to infinity except the source vertex, which is set to zero. In
each iteration, the algorithm checks if any edge can be relaxed to

improve the distance to its endpoint. If so, the distance is updated
in the distance array. The algorithm repeats this process for V-1
iterations, where V is the number of vertices in the graph. If a
shorter path is found in the V-th iteration, then the graph has a
negative weight cycle.

Here is an example implementation of the Bellman-Ford algorithm
in Java:

```java
public class BellmanFord {
    public int[] bellmanFord(Graph graph, int source) {
        int[] distance = new int[graph.getVertices()];
        Arrays.fill(distance, Integer.MAX_VALUE);
        distance[source] = 0;

        for (int i = 0; i < graph.getVertices() - 1; i++) {
            for (Edge edge : graph.getEdges()) {
                int u = edge.getSource();
                int v = edge.getDestination();
                int weight = edge.getWeight();
                if (distance[u] != Integer.MAX_VALUE && distance[u]
                    + weight < distance[v]) {
                    distance[v] = distance[u] + weight;
                }
            }
        }

        for (Edge edge : graph.getEdges()) {
            int u = edge.getSource();
            int v = edge.getDestination();
            int weight = edge.getWeight();
            if (distance[u] != Integer.MAX_VALUE && distance[u] +
                weight < distance[v]) {
                System.out.println("Graph contains negative weight
                    cycle");
            }
        }

        return distance;
    }
}
```

In this implementation, the bellmanFord method takes as input
a weighted directed graph and a source vertex. It initializes a
distance array to store the current shortest distance from the source
vertex to each vertex in the graph, and sets all distances to infinity
except the source vertex, which is set to zero. It then iterates
through the graph V-1 times, relaxing each edge in the graph to
improve the distance to its endpoint. Finally, it checks for negative
weight cycles by iterating through the edges one more time. The
method returns the distance array.

The Bellman-Ford algorithm can be used in a variety of applications, such as finding the shortest path in a network, detecting negative weight cycles in a graph, and solving the shortest path problem in a road network. However, its time complexity of O(VE) makes it less efficient than other algorithms such as Dijkstra's algorithm for certain use cases.

3.17 How can you detect a cycle in a linked list? Describe the Floyd's Cycle-Finding algorithm.

Detecting a cycle in a linked list is an important problem in computer science. One commonly used algorithm for cycle detection is Floyd's Cycle-Finding algorithm, also known as the "tortoise and hare" algorithm. The basic idea behind this algorithm is to use two pointers, one moving faster than the other, to traverse the linked list. If there is a cycle in the linked list, then the faster pointer will eventually catch up to the slower pointer and they will meet at a point in the cycle.

Here is an example implementation of Floyd's Cycle-Finding algorithm in Java:

```java
public boolean hasCycle(ListNode head) {
    if (head == null || head.next == null) {
        return false;
    }
    ListNode slow = head;
    ListNode fast = head.next;
    while (slow != fast) {
        if (fast == null || fast.next == null) {
            return false;
        }
        slow = slow.next;
        fast = fast.next.next;
    }
    return true;
}
```

In this implementation, the hasCycle method takes as input the head node of a linked list and returns true if the linked list contains a cycle, and false otherwise. It initializes two pointers, slow and fast, to the head of the linked list. It then iterates through the linked list, with the slow pointer moving one step at a time and the fast pointer moving two steps at a time. If there is a cycle in the linked list, then the fast pointer will eventually catch up to the slow pointer and they will meet at a point in the cycle. If there is no cycle, then the fast pointer will reach the end of the linked list before the slow pointer catches up to it.

The time complexity of Floyd's Cycle-Finding algorithm is $O(n)$, where n is the length of the linked list. The space complexity is $O(1)$, as the algorithm only requires two pointers to traverse the linked list.

3.18 What is the Union-Find data structure, and how can it be used to solve the Disjoint Set problem?

The Union-Find data structure, also known as the Disjoint Set data structure, is a data structure that keeps track of a collection of disjoint sets. It provides two primary operations, union and find, which can be used to merge two sets and determine whether two elements belong to the same set, respectively. The Union-Find data structure is useful for solving a variety of problems involving connectivity, such as finding connected components in a graph or detecting cycles in an undirected graph.

The Disjoint Set problem is the problem of determining whether a set of n elements can be partitioned into non-overlapping subsets. The Union-Find data structure can be used to solve this problem by maintaining a collection of disjoint sets and merging them as necessary to create larger sets. Initially, each element is in its own set. The union operation is used to merge two sets, and the find operation is used to determine which set an element belongs to.

Here is an example implementation of the Union-Find data structure in Java:

```java
public class UnionFind {
    private int[] parent;
    private int[] rank;

    public UnionFind(int n) {
        parent = new int[n];
        rank = new int[n];
        for (int i = 0; i < n; i++) {
            parent[i] = i;
```

```
        }
    }

    public int find(int x) {
        if (parent[x] != x) {
            parent[x] = find(parent[x]);
        }
        return parent[x];
    }

    public void union(int x, int y) {
        int rootX = find(x);
        int rootY = find(y);
        if (rootX != rootY) {
            if (rank[rootX] < rank[rootY]) {
                parent[rootX] = rootY;
            } else if (rank[rootX] > rank[rootY]) {
                parent[rootY] = rootX;
            } else {
                parent[rootY] = rootX;
                rank[rootX]++;
            }
        }
    }
}
```

In this implementation, the UnionFind class represents a Union-Find data structure. It contains two arrays, parent and rank, which are used to keep track of the parent of each element and the rank of each set, respectively. The find method returns the root of the set that contains the given element, and the union method merges two sets by setting the root of one set to be the parent of the root of the other set.

The time complexity of the find and union operations in the Union-Find data structure is O(alpha(n)), where alpha is the inverse Ackermann function and n is the number of elements in the data structure. This makes the Union-Find data structure efficient for solving the Disjoint Set problem and other connectivity problems in graphs.

3.19 Describe the KMP (Knuth-Morris-Pratt) algorithm and its use in pattern searching within a string.

The Knuth-Morris-Pratt (KMP) algorithm is a string searching algorithm that is used to find occurrences of a pattern within a larger string. The algorithm achieves this by preprocessing the pattern to construct a table of partial matches, which is then used to avoid unnecessary comparisons when searching for the pattern within the larger string.

The KMP algorithm works as follows:

Construct a table of partial matches for the pattern.

- The table is an array lps of the same length as the pattern.

- The value lps[i] at index i represents the length of the longest proper suffix of the substring pattern[0:i] that is also a prefix of the same substring.

- The value of lps[0] is always 0, as a string of length 1 has no proper suffix.

Use the lps table to search for the pattern within the larger string.

- Initialize two pointers, i and j, to 0 and 0, respectively.

- While i is less than the length of the larger string:

- If the character at index i of the larger string matches the character at index j of the pattern, increment both i and j.

- If j is equal to the length of the pattern, then a match has been found and the index of the first occurrence of the pattern within the larger string is i - j.

- If the character at index i of the larger string does not match the character at index j of the pattern:

- If j is equal to 0, increment i.

- Otherwise, set j to lps[j-1].

The KMP algorithm is particularly useful when searching for a pattern within a large string, as it can avoid unnecessary comparisons by using the lps table to skip over parts of the larger string that are guaranteed not to match the pattern. This makes the algorithm more efficient than other naive string searching algorithms, such as the brute-force method of comparing each possible substring of the larger string with the pattern.

Here is an example implementation of the KMP algorithm in Java:

```java
public static List<Integer> kmp(String text, String pattern) {
    List<Integer> indices = new ArrayList<Integer>();
    int n = text.length();
    int m = pattern.length();
    int[] lps = computeLPS(pattern);
    int i = 0, j = 0;
    while (i < n) {
        if (text.charAt(i) == pattern.charAt(j)) {
            i++;
            j++;
            if (j == m) {
                indices.add(i - j);
                j = lps[j - 1];
            }
        } else if (j > 0) {
            j = lps[j - 1];
        } else {
            i++;
        }
    }
    return indices;
}

private static int[] computeLPS(String pattern) {
    int m = pattern.length();
    int[] lps = new int[m];
    int i = 1, j = 0;
    while (i < m) {
        if (pattern.charAt(i) == pattern.charAt(j)) {
            j++;
            lps[i] = j;
            i++;
        } else if (j > 0) {
            j = lps[j - 1];
        } else {
            lps[i] = 0;
            i++;
        }
    }
    return lps;
}
```

In this implementation, the kmp method takes as input a larger string text and a pattern string pattern, and

3.20 What is the concept of greedy algorithms, and how do they differ from other algorithmic approaches? Provide an example of a problem solved using a greedy algorithm.

A greedy algorithm is an algorithmic paradigm that makes the locally optimal choice at each step in the hope of finding a global optimum solution. In other words, the algorithm chooses the best option available at the current moment without worrying about the future implications of that choice. Greedy algorithms are typically simple, efficient, and easy to implement.

One of the key characteristics of greedy algorithms is that they do not necessarily always produce the optimal solution. In some cases, a greedy approach may lead to a suboptimal solution that is still reasonably good but not the best possible outcome. In other cases, a greedy approach may fail to find any solution at all.

A classic example of a problem that can be solved using a greedy algorithm is the fractional knapsack problem. In this problem, we are given a set of items, each with a weight and a value, and a knapsack that can hold a certain weight limit. The goal is to fill the knapsack with items that maximize the total value while respecting the weight limit.

The greedy approach to this problem involves sorting the items by their value-to-weight ratio and then adding items to the knapsack in descending order of this ratio until the knapsack is full. This approach works because it selects the most valuable items first, while still respecting the weight limit.

Here's an example implementation of the fractional knapsack problem in Java:

```java
public static double fractionalKnapsack(int[] values, int[] weights,
    int capacity) {
    int n = values.length;
    double[] ratios = new double[n];
    for (int i = 0; i < n; i++) {
        ratios[i] = (double) values[i] / weights[i];
    }
    double maxVal = 0.0;
```

```
while (capacity > 0 && maxRatio > 0) {
    int index = getMaxRatioIndex(ratios);
    if (weights[index] <= capacity) {
        maxVal += values[index];
        capacity -= weights[index];
    } else {
        maxVal += ratios[index] * capacity;
        capacity = 0;
    }
    ratios[index] = 0;
}
return maxVal;
}

private static int getMaxRatioIndex(double[] ratios) {
    int maxIndex = 0;
    double maxRatio = 0;
    for (int i = 0; i < ratios.length; i++) {
        if (ratios[i] > maxRatio) {
            maxRatio = ratios[i];
            maxIndex = i;
        }
    }
    return maxIndex;
}
```

In this implementation, the fractionalKnapsack method takes as input an array of item values values, an array of item weights weights, and the capacity of the knapsack capacity. The method first computes the value-to-weight ratios of all the items and then repeatedly selects the item with the highest ratio until the knapsack is full or there are no more items left. The getMaxRatioIndex method is a helper method that returns the index of the item with the highest ratio. The method returns the maximum total value that can be obtained from the items that fit in the knapsack.

Overall, the greedy approach to the fractional knapsack problem is efficient and provides a good approximate solution to the problem. However, it does not always produce the optimal solution in all cases, and there may be other algorithmic approaches that provide better results in some scenarios.

Chapter 4

Advanced

4.1 Can you explain the A* search algorithm and its applications in pathfinding and AI?

The A* search algorithm is a pathfinding algorithm used to find the shortest path between two nodes in a weighted graph. It is a variant of Dijkstra's algorithm, but with the addition of a heuristic function that estimates the cost of the cheapest path from the current node to the goal node.

The algorithm works by maintaining a set of open nodes, representing nodes that still need to be explored, and a set of closed nodes, representing nodes that have already been explored. At each step, the algorithm selects the node in the open set with the lowest cost estimate, which is the sum of the cost of the path from the starting node to the current node and the heuristic estimate of the remaining cost to the goal node. The algorithm then expands the selected node and adds its neighbors to the open set if they have not been visited before or if a better path has been found.

The heuristic function used in A* is typically an admissible heuristic, meaning that it never overestimates the actual cost of reaching the goal node. One commonly used heuristic for pathfinding is the

Manhattan distance, which calculates the distance between two nodes as the sum of the absolute differences between their x and y coordinates.

A* search algorithm is widely used in computer games and AI applications for pathfinding, as it is efficient and can handle complex environments with many obstacles and variable costs. It is also used in robotics for motion planning, in natural language processing for parsing, and in many other areas where finding the optimal path is important.

Here's an example implementation of the A* search algorithm in Java:

```java
public List<Node> aStarSearch(Node start, Node goal) {
    PriorityQueue<Node> openSet = new PriorityQueue<>();
    Set<Node> closedSet = new HashSet<>();
    Map<Node, Node> cameFrom = new HashMap<>();
    Map<Node, Double> gScore = new HashMap<>();
    Map<Node, Double> fScore = new HashMap<>();

    gScore.put(start, 0.0);
    fScore.put(start, heuristic(start, goal));
    openSet.add(start);

    while (!openSet.isEmpty()) {
        Node current = openSet.poll();
        if (current.equals(goal)) {
            return reconstructPath(cameFrom, current);
        }

        closedSet.add(current);
        for (Edge neighbor : current.getNeighbors()) {
            Node neighborNode = neighbor.getDestination();
            if (closedSet.contains(neighborNode)) {
                continue;
            }
            double tentativeGScore = gScore.get(current) + neighbor.
                getWeight();
            if (!openSet.contains(neighborNode) || tentativeGScore <
                gScore.get(neighborNode)) {
                cameFrom.put(neighborNode, current);
                gScore.put(neighborNode, tentativeGScore);
                fScore.put(neighborNode, tentativeGScore + heuristic
                    (neighborNode, goal));
                if (!openSet.contains(neighborNode)) {
                    openSet.add(neighborNode);
                }
            }
        }
    }

    return null;
}

private double heuristic(Node node, Node goal) {
    return Math.abs(node.getX() - goal.getX()) + Math.abs(node.getY
```

```
        () - goal.getY());
}

private List<Node> reconstructPath(Map<Node, Node> cameFrom, Node
      current) {
    List<Node> path = new ArrayList<>();
    path.add(current);
    while (cameFrom.containsKey(current)) {
        current = cameFrom.get(current);
        path.add(0, current);
    }
    return path;
}
```

In this implementation, the aStarSearch method takes as input a starting node start and a goal node goal. The method initializes the open set with the starting node, and the closed set is initially empty. The heuristic method calculates the Manhattan distance between two nodes.

4.2 What is a Bloom filter, and in which situations is it useful?

A Bloom filter is a probabilistic data structure used to test whether an element is a member of a set. It is a space-efficient data structure that provides a way to trade off memory usage for the probability of false positives.

The Bloom filter is essentially an array of bits, initialized to zero. To insert an element into the Bloom filter, a set of hash functions are applied to the element's value, and the resulting positions in the array are set to one. To test whether an element is in the set, the same hash functions are applied to the element's value, and the corresponding positions in the array are checked. If all of the positions are set to one, the element is likely to be in the set, but there is a small probability of false positives.

The key advantage of Bloom filters is their space efficiency. They can represent a large set with a small amount of memory, and the size of the filter can be adjusted to control the probability of false positives. This makes them useful in situations where the space is limited, and false positives are acceptable.

Bloom filters are commonly used in network routing and caching, where they can be used to reduce the number of expensive lookups to a remote server or database. They are also used in spell checking, malware detection, and duplicate elimination in databases.

Here's an example implementation of a Bloom filter in Java:

```java
public class BloomFilter {
    private final int[] bits;
    private final int k;
    private final HashFunction[] hashFunctions;

    public BloomFilter(int m, int k, HashFunction... hashFunctions)
        {
        this.bits = new int[m];
        this.k = k;
        this.hashFunctions = hashFunctions;
    }

    public void add(String value) {
        for (HashFunction hashFunction : hashFunctions) {
            int index = hashFunction.hash(value) % bits.length;
            bits[index]++;
        }
    }

    public boolean contains(String value) {
        for (HashFunction hashFunction : hashFunctions) {
            int index = hashFunction.hash(value) % bits.length;
            if (bits[index] == 0) {
                return false;
            }
        }
        return true;
    }

    public int size() {
        return bits.length;
    }

    public int count() {
        int count = 0;
        for (int bit : bits) {
            if (bit > 0) {
                count++;
            }
        }
        return count;
    }

    public double falsePositiveProbability() {
        double p = 1.0;
        for (int i = 0; i < k; i++) {
            p *= 1 - (double) count() / size();
        }
        return 1 - Math.pow(p, k);
    }
}

public interface HashFunction {
    int hash(String value);
```

```
}

public class MurmurHash implements HashFunction {
    private final int seed;

    public MurmurHash(int seed) {
        this.seed = seed;
    }

    @Override
    public int hash(String value) {
        return MurmurHash3.murmurhash3_x86_32(value.getBytes(), 0,
            value.length(), seed);
    }
}
```

In this implementation, the BloomFilter class represents a Bloom filter with a given size m, number of hash functions k, and array of hash functions hashFunctions. The add method adds a string value to the filter by applying each hash function to the value and setting the corresponding bit in the array. The contains method checks if a string value is likely to be in the filter by applying each hash function to the value and checking if the corresponding bits in the array are set. The size method returns the size of the filter,

4.3   Describe the concept of a self-balancing binary search tree, and explain how an AVL tree and a Red-Black tree work.

A self-balancing binary search tree is a binary search tree that automatically adjusts its structure to maintain a balanced tree, ensuring efficient search, insertion, and deletion operations. The goal of a self-balancing binary search tree is to maintain a balance between the left and right subtrees of each node, preventing one subtree from being significantly deeper than the other.

AVL trees and Red-Black trees are two commonly used types of self-balancing binary search trees.

AVL Tree: An AVL tree is a self-balancing binary search tree in which the height of the left and right subtrees of each node differs by at most one. To maintain this property, the AVL tree uses a balancing operation called a rotation. A rotation is a local transformation that preserves the order of the tree but changes the structure of the tree by rearranging nodes.

When a node is inserted into an AVL tree, the tree is checked for balance. If the height of the left and right subtrees of a node differs by more than one, a rotation is performed to balance the tree. AVL trees can perform both left and right rotations, which can be single or double rotations depending on the structure of the tree.

Here is an example of an AVL tree insertion operation:

```
// insert 4 into the following AVL tree
//      6
//     / \
//    3   9
//   / \
//  1   5

// After insertion:
//        6
//       / \
//      4   9
//     / \
//    3   5
//   /
//1


AVLNode insert(AVLNode root, int value) {
    if (root == null) {
        return new AVLNode(value);
    }

    if (value < root.value) {
        root.left = insert(root.left, value);
    } else {
        root.right = insert(root.right, value);
    }

    int balance = getBalance(root);

    if (balance > 1 && value < root.left.value) {
        return rightRotate(root);
    }

    if (balance < -1 && value > root.right.value) {
        return leftRotate(root);
    }

    if (balance > 1 && value > root.left.value) {
        root.left = leftRotate(root.left);
        return rightRotate(root);
    }

    if (balance < -1 && value < root.right.value) {
        root.right = rightRotate(root.right);
        return leftRotate(root);
    }
```

```
        return root;
}

int getHeight(AVLNode node) {
    if (node == null) {
        return 0;
    }

    return Math.max(getHeight(node.left), getHeight(node.right)) +
        1;
}

int getBalance(AVLNode node) {
    if (node == null) {
        return 0;
    }

    return getHeight(node.left) - getHeight(node.right);
}

AVLNode rightRotate(AVLNode y) {
    AVLNode x = y.left;
    AVLNode T2 = x.right;

    x.right = y;
    y.left = T2;

    return x;
}

AVLNode leftRotate(AVLNode x) {
    AVLNode y = x.right;
    AVLNode T2 = y.left;

    y.left = x;
    x.right = T2;

    return y;
}
```

Red-Black Tree: A Red-Black tree is another type of self-balancing binary search tree. It maintains a balance between the left and right subtrees of each node by coloring each node either red or black. The color of the node determines the balance of the tree, and the structure of the tree is adjusted to maintain a balance when new nodes are added or removed.

4.4   Explain the Boyer-Moore string search algorithm and how it improves upon the naive string search approach.

The Boyer-Moore string search algorithm is a fast and efficient algorithm for finding occurrences of a pattern within a string. It improves upon the naive string search approach by reducing the number of character comparisons needed to search for the pattern.

The algorithm works by first preprocessing the pattern to generate two tables, the "bad character" table and the "good suffix" table. The bad character table indicates the maximum shift distance for a given character in the pattern. The good suffix table indicates the maximum shift distance for a given suffix of the pattern.

When searching for the pattern within the string, the algorithm starts from the end of the pattern and compares the last character of the pattern with the corresponding character in the string. If there is a mismatch, the algorithm uses the bad character table to determine the maximum shift distance based on the last occurrence of the mismatched character in the pattern. If the character is not found in the pattern, the entire pattern can be shifted by the length of the pattern.

If the last character matches, the algorithm compares the second to last characters, and so on until the entire pattern is matched or a mismatch is found. If a mismatch is found, the algorithm uses the good suffix table to determine the maximum shift distance based on the longest matching suffix of the pattern.

Here is an example implementation of the Boyer-Moore algorithm in Java:

```java
public static List<Integer> boyerMoore(String pattern, String text)
    {
    List<Integer> matches = new ArrayList<>();

    int n = text.length();
    int m = pattern.length();

    // preprocessing bad character table
    int[] badChar = new int[256];
    Arrays.fill(badChar, -1);
    for (int i = 0; i < m; i++) {
        badChar[pattern.charAt(i)] = i;
    }
```

```
// preprocessing good suffix table
int[] goodSuffix = new int[m];
Arrays.fill(goodSuffix, m);
int i = m - 1;
int j = m - 2;
while (i >= 0 && j >= 0) {
    if (pattern.charAt(i) == pattern.charAt(j)) {
        goodSuffix[j] = i;
        i--;
        j--;
    } else {
        i = m - 1;
        j--;
    }
}
for (int k = 0; k < m - 1; k++) {
    int r = m - 2 - k;
    int shift = m - goodSuffix[r];
    if (goodSuffix[r] != m && pattern.charAt(r) != pattern.
        charAt(m - 1)) {
        shift = Math.max(shift, m - 1 - badChar[pattern.charAt(r
            )]);
    }
    goodSuffix[k] = shift;
}

// searching for matches
int k = m - 1;
while (k < n) {
    int j = m - 1;
    int i = k;
    while (j >= 0 && text.charAt(i) == pattern.charAt(j)) {
        i--;
        j--;
    }
    if (j < 0) {
        matches.add(i + 1);
        k++;
    } else {
        int shift = Math.max(goodSuffix[j], j - badChar[text.
            charAt(i)]);
        k += shift;
    }
}

return matches;
}
```

Overall, the Boyer-Moore algorithm is a powerful and efficient string search algorithm that can greatly improve the performance of pattern searching in many applications.

4.5 Describe the B-tree and B+ tree data structures, and discuss their applications in databases and file systems.

B-trees and B+ trees are self-balancing tree data structures commonly used in databases and file systems to efficiently store and retrieve large amounts of data. They differ in their structure and usage, but both provide efficient and fast access to data.

A B-tree is a tree data structure that maintains data in a sorted order. The tree consists of a root node, internal nodes, and leaf nodes. Each node contains a certain number of keys and pointers to its children. The keys in each node are ordered from left to right, and the number of keys in each node is typically between a minimum and maximum value. B-trees are designed to balance themselves dynamically as new data is added or removed, ensuring that the tree remains efficient for searching, insertion, and deletion operations. B-trees are commonly used in databases to index and organize data, as well as in file systems to manage file data.

A B+ tree is a variation of the B-tree that is specifically designed for use in databases and file systems. Like the B-tree, a B+ tree is a tree data structure that maintains data in a sorted order, but it differs in the way it stores and retrieves data. In a B+ tree, all data is stored in the leaf nodes, while the internal nodes only contain pointers to the child nodes. This allows for more efficient disk access, as a single read operation can access a larger amount of data. B+ trees are also designed to minimize the number of disk accesses needed to retrieve a certain range of data, making them ideal for use in database indexing and file systems.

Here is an example of a B+ tree with a degree of 3:

```
              [20, 30, 40]
            /    |    |    \
[5, 10, 15]   [20]  [30, 35]  [40, 45, 50]
```

In this example, the internal nodes contain 2 to 3 keys and 3 to 4 pointers to child nodes. The leaf nodes contain 1 to 2 keys and pointers to the actual data. Searches, insertions, and deletions in a B+ tree are typically performed by recursively traversing the tree from the root node to the leaf nodes, where the actual data is stored.

Both B-trees and B+ trees have significant advantages over other data structures when dealing with large amounts of data, particularly in the context of databases and file systems. They offer efficient search and retrieval operations, and can be optimized for specific use cases through careful tuning of the degree and other parameters. B-trees and B+ trees remain popular and widely used data structures in modern computing applications.

4.6 What is the Maximum Subarray Problem, and how can the Kadane's algorithm be used to solve it?

The Maximum Subarray Problem is a classic algorithmic problem that involves finding the contiguous subarray within a one-dimensional array that has the largest sum. In other words, given an array of integers, we want to find a subarray of contiguous elements that have the largest sum.

For example, given the input array [-2, 1, -3, 4, -1, 2, 1, -5, 4], the subarray [4, -1, 2, 1] has the largest sum of 6.

Kadane's algorithm is a simple and efficient algorithm for solving the Maximum Subarray Problem. It works by iterating through the array and maintaining two variables: the maximum subarray sum seen so far, and the maximum subarray sum ending at the current position. The maximum subarray sum ending at the current position is either the current element itself, or the sum of the current element and the maximum subarray sum ending at the previous position.

Here is an implementation of Kadane's algorithm in Java:

```java
public int maxSubarraySum(int[] nums) {
    int maxSoFar = nums[0];
    int maxEndingHere = nums[0];
    for (int i = 1; i < nums.length; i++) {
        maxEndingHere = Math.max(nums[i], maxEndingHere + nums[i]);
        maxSoFar = Math.max(maxSoFar, maxEndingHere);
    }
    return maxSoFar;
}
```

In this implementation, the variable maxSoFar stores the largest sum seen so far, and maxEndingHere stores the largest sum ending at the current position. The for loop iterates through the array, updating maxEndingHere and maxSoFar as necessary. The final value of maxSoFar is the largest sum found.

Kadane's algorithm has a time complexity of O(n), making it an efficient solution to the Maximum Subarray Problem. It is widely used in practice, particularly in applications that involve large amounts of numerical data, such as image and signal processing, finance, and scientific computing.

4.7 Can you explain the concept of backtracking and provide an example of an algorithm that uses backtracking?

Backtracking is an algorithmic technique that involves recursively trying out different solutions to a problem, and undoing solutions that don't work until a valid solution is found. Backtracking is useful when we need to explore all possible solutions to a problem, such as in combinatorial problems, optimization problems, or constraint satisfaction problems.

The basic idea behind backtracking is to build a solution incrementally, one step at a time, and test whether the partial solution is valid at each step. If the partial solution is valid, we continue to the next step. If the partial solution is not valid, we undo the previous step and try a different solution.

Here is an example of a problem that can be solved using backtracking: the N-Queens problem. The N-Queens problem involves placing N queens on an NxN chessboard such that no two queens attack each other. In other words, no two queens should be in the same row, column, or diagonal.

Here is an implementation of the N-Queens problem using backtracking in Java:

```
public List<List<String>> solveNQueens(int n) {
    List<List<String>> results = new ArrayList<>();
    int[] queens = new int[n];
```

```java
        Arrays.fill(queens, -1);
        backtrack(results, queens, 0);
        return results;
    }

    private void backtrack(List<List<String>> results, int[] queens, int
        row) {
        if (row == queens.length) {
            results.add(buildBoard(queens));
            return;
        }
        for (int col = 0; col < queens.length; col++) {
            if (isValid(queens, row, col)) {
                queens[row] = col;
                backtrack(results, queens, row+1);
                queens[row] = -1;
            }
        }
    }

    private boolean isValid(int[] queens, int row, int col) {
        for (int i = 0; i < row; i++) {
            int j = queens[i];
            if (j == col || Math.abs(j - col) == Math.abs(i - row)) {
                return false;
            }
        }
        return true;
    }

    private List<String> buildBoard(int[] queens) {
        List<String> board = new ArrayList<>();
        for (int i = 0; i < queens.length; i++) {
            char[] row = new char[queens.length];
            Arrays.fill(row, '.');
            row[queens[i]] = 'Q';
            board.add(new String(row));
        }
        return board;
    }
```

In this implementation, the solveNQueens method initializes an array of integers queens to represent the columns where the queens are placed. The backtrack method recursively tries out different solutions by iterating through the columns of the current row, and checking if each placement of the queen is valid using the isValid method. If a valid placement is found, the method calls itself recursively on the next row. If no valid placement is found, the method backtracks to the previous row and tries a different placement. When a valid solution is found, the buildBoard method constructs a list of strings to represent the board.

Backtracking can be a powerful technique for solving complex problems, but it can also be computationally expensive since it involves exploring all possible solutions. Therefore, it is important to carefully design the backtracking algorithm to avoid exploring unnecessary solutions, and to use other optimization techniques when possible.

4.8 What is the Minimum Spanning Tree (MST) problem, and how do Kruskal's and Prim's algorithms solve it?

The Minimum Spanning Tree (MST) problem is a well-known graph problem that involves finding the minimum cost tree that spans all nodes in a given graph. In other words, the MST problem asks for the subset of edges in a graph that form a tree, connecting all the vertices while minimizing the sum of edge weights.

Kruskal's algorithm and Prim's algorithm are two popular algorithms for solving the MST problem.

Kruskal's algorithm works by sorting all edges in ascending order of their weights and then adding them to the MST one by one, as long as the edge being added does not create a cycle. This is done by maintaining a set of disjoint subsets, initially containing each vertex as a separate subset. As each edge is considered, its endpoints are placed into the same subset if they are not already in the same set. If the endpoints are already in the same set, the edge would form a cycle and is discarded.

Here is an example implementation of Kruskal's algorithm in Java:

```java
public static List<Edge> kruskalMST(Graph g) {
    List<Edge> mst = new ArrayList<>();
    List<Edge> edges = new ArrayList<>(g.getEdges());
    Collections.sort(edges); // sort edges by weight
    DisjointSet ds = new DisjointSet(g.getVertices());

    for (Edge e : edges) {
        int u = e.getSource();
        int v = e.getDestination();
        int setU = ds.find(u);
        int setV = ds.find(v);
        if (setU != setV) { // check if adding edge creates a cycle
            mst.add(e);
            ds.union(setU, setV); // merge the two subsets
        }
    }
    return mst;
}
```

Prim's algorithm, on the other hand, works by building the MST incrementally from a starting vertex, adding the minimum weight edge that connects the already visited vertices to the unvisited vertices in each iteration. This process continues until all vertices are visited.

Here is an example implementation of Prim's algorithm in Java:

```java
public static List<Edge> primMST(Graph g) {
    List<Edge> mst = new ArrayList<>();
    int[] parent = new int[g.getNumVertices()];
    int[] key = new int[g.getNumVertices()];
    boolean[] mstSet = new boolean[g.getNumVertices()];
    Arrays.fill(key, Integer.MAX_VALUE);
    key[0] = 0;
    parent[0] = -1;

    for (int i = 0; i < g.getNumVertices() - 1; i++) {
        int u = minKey(key, mstSet);
        mstSet[u] = true;
        for (Edge e : g.getAdjacentEdges(u)) {
            int v = e.getDestination();
            if (!mstSet[v] && e.getWeight() < key[v]) {
                parent[v] = u;
                key[v] = e.getWeight();
            }
        }
    }

    for (int i = 1; i < g.getNumVertices(); i++) {
        mst.add(new Edge(parent[i], i, key[i]));
    }
    return mst;
}

private static int minKey(int[] key, boolean[] mstSet) {
    int min = Integer.MAX_VALUE, minIndex = -1;
    for (int i = 0; i < key.length; i++) {
        if (!mstSet[i] && key[i] < min) {
            min = key[i];
            minIndex = i;
        }
    }
    return minIndex;
}
```

4.9 Describe the concept of load balancing and its importance in distributed systems.

Load balancing is the process of distributing workloads across multiple computing resources, such as servers or clusters, in order to optimize performance, increase reliability, and improve efficiency. In distributed systems, load balancing is essential to ensure that all resources are used efficiently and effectively, and that the system as a whole is able to handle large volumes of traffic without experiencing downtime or performance issues.

Load balancing can be achieved through various techniques, including:

Round-robin load balancing: this technique distributes requests equally across all available resources, so each resource takes an equal share of the workload.

Weighted load balancing: this technique assigns different weights to each resource based on its processing power, so that more powerful resources can handle larger workloads.

Least-connections load balancing: this technique assigns incoming requests to the resource with the fewest active connections, in order to prevent overloading of any single resource.

IP hash load balancing: this technique assigns incoming requests to resources based on their IP addresses, in order to ensure that requests from the same IP address are always handled by the same resource.

Load balancing is particularly important in distributed systems that involve high-volume transaction processing or web applications, where the workload can be highly variable and unpredictable. By distributing the workload across multiple resources, load balancing helps to ensure that the system can handle large volumes of traffic without slowing down or crashing, and can also provide fault tolerance by ensuring that if one resource fails, the workload can be automatically redirected to another available resource.

Load balancing can be implemented using various tools and technologies, including hardware load balancers, software-based load balancers, and cloud-based load balancing services. Each of these approaches has its own advantages and disadvantages, depending on the specific requirements of the system and the workload.

4.10 Explain the Counting Sort and Radix Sort algorithms, and discuss their time complexity and use cases.

Counting Sort and Radix Sort are two commonly used sorting algorithms that have different strengths and use cases.

Counting Sort: Counting Sort is a simple sorting algorithm that works well when the range of input values is relatively small. The algorithm works by counting the number of occurrences of each input value, and then using this information to determine the correct order of the input elements. For example, suppose we have an array of integers ranging from 0 to 9, and we want to sort it using Counting Sort. We would first create a count array with 10 elements, one for each possible input value. Then, we would iterate through the input array, incrementing the count array at the appropriate index for each input value. Finally, we would iterate through the count array, adding each index to the output array the number of times indicated by its value. The time complexity of Counting Sort is $O(n + k)$, where n is the number of input elements and k is the range of input values. Counting Sort is particularly useful for sorting large sets of integers with a small range of values, such as counting frequencies of characters in a string.

Radix Sort: Radix Sort is a non-comparison-based sorting algorithm that works by sorting elements one digit at a time. The algorithm works by first sorting elements by their least significant digit, and then continuing to sort by increasingly significant digits until all elements are sorted. For example, suppose we have an array of integers ranging from 1 to 1000, and we want to sort it using Radix Sort. We would first sort the array by the ones digit, creating 10 buckets (0-9) for each digit, and then concatenate the elements in each bucket to form a new array. We would then repeat this process for the tens digit and the hundreds digit until the array is fully sorted. The time complexity of Radix Sort is $O(d(n + k))$, where d is the number of digits in the largest input value, n is the number of input elements, and k is the range of input values. Radix Sort is particularly useful for sorting large sets of integers with a large range of values, such as sorting IP addresses or sorting large integers used in cryptography.

In summary, Counting Sort is a simple and efficient algorithm for sorting a small range of input values, while Radix Sort is a non-comparison-based algorithm that works well for sorting a large range of input values with a fixed number of digits. The choice of algorithm will depend on the specific use case and the characteristics of the input data.

4.11   What is the Traveling Salesman Problem, and how can it be approximated using heuristics or optimization techniques?

The Traveling Salesman Problem (TSP) is a classic optimization problem in computer science, which seeks to find the shortest possible route that visits each of a given set of cities exactly once and then returns to the starting city. It is a well-known NP-hard problem, meaning that it is computationally infeasible to solve exactly for large input sizes.

Heuristic algorithms are often used to approximate solutions to the TSP. One such algorithm is the nearest neighbor algorithm, which starts at a randomly chosen city and repeatedly chooses the nearest unvisited city until all cities have been visited. While this algorithm is simple and easy to implement, it often produces suboptimal solutions.

Another heuristic algorithm for the TSP is the 2-opt algorithm, which iteratively improves an initial tour by swapping pairs of edges that cross each other. This algorithm can also be extended to the k-opt algorithm, which considers larger sets of edges to swap, and can produce even better solutions.

Metaheuristic algorithms, such as simulated annealing and genetic algorithms, can also be used to solve the TSP. These algorithms start with an initial solution and iteratively modify it by applying random perturbations and accepting improvements, with the aim of finding a global optimum.

In addition to heuristics and metaheuristics, there are also exact optimization techniques that can be used to solve small instances of the TSP. One such technique is dynamic programming, which can be used to compute the optimal solution for instances with up to a few dozen cities.

Overall, the TSP is an important problem in computer science and operations research, with applications in logistics, transportation, and other fields where routing and scheduling are important. While exact solutions are often infeasible for large instances, heuristic and optimization techniques can be used to find good approximate solutions.

4.12 Describe the Strassen's Matrix Multiplication algorithm and its time complexity.

Strassen's matrix multiplication algorithm is an algorithm for multiplying two matrices. It was proposed by Volker Strassen in 1969 and is notable for its lower time complexity than the standard matrix multiplication algorithm.

The standard algorithm for multiplying two n x n matrices has a time complexity of $O(n^3)$. Strassen's algorithm improves on this by dividing each matrix into four submatrices of size n/2 x n/2, recursively computing the products of these submatrices using seven matrix multiplications, and then combining these products to obtain the final result.

The time complexity of Strassen's algorithm is given by the recurrence relation $T(n) = 7T(n/2) + O(n^2)$, which can be solved to give a time complexity of $O(n^{log2(7)})O(n^2.81)$. Thus, Strassen's algorithm is more efficient than the standard algorithm for large values of n.

Here is an example of how Strassen's algorithm works for multiplying two 2 x 2 matrices:

Consider the matrices A and B:

```
A = | a11   a12 |
    | a21   a22 |

B = | b11   b12 |
    | b21   b22 |
```

We can divide each matrix into four submatrices of size 1 x 1:

```
A = | A11   A12 |    B = | B11   B12 |
    | A21   A22 |        | B21   B22 |
```

We can then compute seven products of these submatrices:

```
P1 = A11 * (B12 - B22)
P2 = (A11 + A12) * B22
P3 = (A21 + A22) * B11
P4 = A22 * (B21 - B11)
P5 = (A11 + A22) * (B11 + B22)
P6 = (A12 - A22) * (B21 + B22)
P7 = (A11 - A21) * (B11 + B12)
```

We can then combine these products to obtain the final result:

```
C11 = P5 + P4 - P2 + P6
C12 = P1 + P2
C21 = P3 + P4
C22 = P5 + P1 - P3 - P7
```

This example illustrates how Strassen's algorithm works by recursively dividing the matrices into submatrices and computing the products of these submatrices using a small number of matrix multiplications. While the algorithm has a lower time complexity than the standard algorithm for large matrices, it requires more memory and is often not used in practice for matrices of small to moderate size.

4.13 Explain the Skip List data structure and its applications in search and storage systems.

The Skip List is a probabilistic data structure that can be used for searching, insertion, and deletion operations. It is similar to a balanced binary search tree, but instead of using rotations to keep the tree balanced, it uses a randomization technique. The Skip List was first introduced by William Pugh in 1990.

A Skip List is a linked list with additional pointers that allow for skipping some elements during search operations. Each node in the list contains a key-value pair, where the key is used for comparison during search operations. The list is organized into levels, with the first level containing all the elements of the list, and each subsequent level containing a subset of the elements from the previous level. The elements in each level are connected by forward pointers that allow for skipping some elements during search operations.

The number of levels in a Skip List is determined probabilistically, with the probability of an element being included in a higher level decreasing exponentially as the level increases. The average number of levels in a Skip List is logarithmic to the number of elements in the list.

The Skip List provides an efficient way to search for an element in a large collection of data. The search time complexity of a Skip List is O(log n), which is comparable to that of a balanced binary search tree. The insertion and deletion operations in a Skip List have the same time complexity as the search operation, with an average case of O(log n).

The Skip List is commonly used in search and storage systems where fast searching and efficient updates are required. It has been used in database indexing, web search engines, and file systems. One advantage of the Skip List is that it does not require any additional memory beyond the data stored in the list, unlike some other data structures such as balanced binary search trees.

4.14 Describe the Rabin-Karp algorithm and its use in string searching.

The Rabin-Karp algorithm is a string searching algorithm that is used to find a pattern within a larger text. It is an efficient algorithm for large texts as it only requires a constant amount of memory, making it ideal for certain applications.

The algorithm works by using a hash function to calculate the hash values of the pattern and the substrings of the text. The hash function used is a rolling hash function, which means that it updates the hash value of a substring in constant time as the substring is shifted by one character.

The Rabin-Karp algorithm then compares the hash values of the pattern and the substrings of the text. If the hash values match, the algorithm checks the pattern and the substring character by character to verify if they are identical. If they match, then the algorithm returns the starting index of the pattern within the text.

The Rabin-Karp algorithm can be implemented using different hash functions, such as the polynomial hash function or the prime hash function. The prime hash function is preferred over the polynomial hash function as it is less likely to produce hash collisions.

The time complexity of the Rabin-Karp algorithm is $O(n+m)$, where n is the length of the text and m is the length of the pattern. However, in the worst case, the algorithm can have a time complexity of $O(nm)$, which occurs when all the hash values of the substrings match the hash value of the pattern, and the algorithm has to verify each match character by character.

An example of the Rabin-Karp algorithm is as follows:

```
// Rabin-Karp algorithm implementation in Java

public class RabinKarp {
    public static int rabinKarp(String text, String pattern) {
        int n = text.length();
        int m = pattern.length();
        int p = 31;  // prime number used for hash function
        int mod = 1000000007;  // modulus used for hash function
        int power = 1;
        int patternHash = 0;
        int[] prefixHash = new int[n+1];
```

```
// calculate the hash value of the pattern
for (int i = 0; i < m; i++) {
    patternHash = (patternHash + (pattern.charAt(i)-'a'+1) *
        power) % mod;
    power = (power * p) % mod;
}

// calculate the prefix hash values of the text
for (int i = 0; i < n; i++) {
    prefixHash[i+1] = (prefixHash[i] + (text.charAt(i)-'a'
        +1) * power) % mod;
    power = (power * p) % mod;
}

// check for matches between the pattern and the substrings
    of the text
for (int i = 0; i <= n-m; i++) {
    int currentHash = (prefixHash[i+m] - prefixHash[i] + mod
        ) % mod;
    if (currentHash == patternHash && text.substring(i, i+m)
        .equals(pattern)) {
        return i;
    }
}

return -1;
}

public static void main(String[] args) {
    String text = "
        abcbcabcabcabcbcabcbcabccbacbabcbcabccbacbabcbcabccbacbabcbcabc
        "
            + "
                cbacbabcbcabccbacbabcbcabccbacbabcbcabccbacb
                ";
    String pattern = "bacb";
    int index = rabinKarp(text, pattern);
    if (index != -1) {
        System.out.println("Pattern found at index " + index);
    } else {
        System.out.println("Pattern not found");
    }
}
}
```

4.15 What is the Edit Distance problem, and how can it be solved using dynamic programming?

The Edit Distance problem, also known as the Levenshtein distance, is the measure of the difference between two strings. The problem involves finding the minimum number of operations (insertions, deletions, or substitutions) required to transform one string into another.

Dynamic programming is a popular technique used to solve the Edit Distance problem. The approach involves building a matrix of size (m+1) x (n+1), where m and n are the lengths of the two strings. The rows and columns of the matrix represent the characters of the two strings, and each cell stores the minimum number of operations required to transform the substring of the first string ending at that position into the substring of the second string ending at that position.

The following steps describe the dynamic programming solution to the Edit Distance problem:

Initialize the first row and column of the matrix with the values from 0 to n and 0 to m, respectively, representing the cost of converting an empty string into a substring of the two strings.

For each cell (i,j) in the matrix, compute the minimum value of the following three cases: a. If the ith character of the first string is equal to the jth character of the second string, the cost of transforming the two substrings is the same as the cost of transforming the substrings ending at (i-1,j-1). b. If the ith character of the first string is different from the jth character of the second string, the cost of transforming the two substrings is the minimum of the cost of inserting, deleting, or substituting the ith character of the first string to match the jth character of the second string, plus the cost of transforming the substrings ending at (i-1,j-1). c. If either i or j is zero, the cost of transforming one of the substrings into an empty string is equal to the length of the other substring.

The final value in the bottom-right corner of the matrix represents the minimum number of operations required to transform the first string into the second string.

The time complexity of the dynamic programming solution to the Edit Distance problem is O(mn), where m and n are the lengths of the two strings. This is because the matrix of size (m+1) x (n+1) needs to be filled in one pass, and each cell requires a constant amount of time to compute.

An example of the dynamic programming solution to the Edit Distance problem for the two strings "kitten" and "sitting" is shown below:

	s	i	t	t	i	n	g
	0	1	2	3	4	5	6
k	1	1	2	3	4	5	6
i	2	1	2	3	4	5	6
t	3	2	1	2	3	4	5
t	4	3	2	1	2	3	4
e	5	4	3	2	2	3	4
n	6	5	4	3	3	2	3

4.16 Explain the concept of a Minimum Cut in a graph and describe the Karger's algorithm for finding an approximate solution.

In graph theory, the minimum cut is defined as the smallest set of edges that, if removed, would disconnect the graph into two or more separate components. It is an important problem in network analysis, particularly in designing robust networks that can resist failures or attacks.

Karger's algorithm, also known as the randomized contraction algorithm, is a randomized algorithm that can find a minimum cut in a graph with high probability. The algorithm works by repeatedly contracting randomly chosen edges until only two nodes remain, which form the cut.

Here is the basic outline of Karger's algorithm:

- Initialize a graph G with n vertices and m edges.

- While there are more than 2 vertices in the graph:

- a. Choose an edge e randomly from the graph.

- b. Contract edge e by merging its two endpoints into a single vertex. This reduces the number of vertices in the graph by 1.

- c. Remove self-loops (if any) resulting from the contraction.

- The remaining two vertices form a cut.

The probability of the algorithm finding the minimum cut is at least $1/n^2$, where n is the number of vertices in the graph. Therefore, running the algorithm multiple times and returning the smallest cut found can increase the probability of finding the actual minimum cut.

Karger's algorithm has a time complexity of $O(n^2 * logn)$ due to the random edge selection process, but it can be improved to $O(m * log^2 n)$ using advanced data structures such as the Fibonacci heap.

Overall, Karger's algorithm provides a simple and effective solution for finding minimum cuts in large graphs, with applications in network design, image segmentation, and clustering.

4.17 What are suffix arrays and suffix trees, and how do they help in solving string-related problems?

Suffix arrays and suffix trees are data structures used to efficiently store and process the suffixes of a given string. Suffixes are the substrings that begin at every possible position in the string and extend to the end of the string.

A suffix array is a sorted array of all the suffixes of a string. Each entry in the suffix array represents the starting position of a suffix in the original string. The suffix array can be constructed in O(n log n) time, where n is the length of the input string, using algorithms like the SA-IS algorithm.

A suffix tree, on the other hand, is a tree-like data structure that represents all the suffixes of a string in a more compact way than a suffix array. The suffix tree can be constructed in linear time, i.e., O(n), using algorithms like the Ukkonen's algorithm.

Suffix arrays and suffix trees can be used to solve various string-related problems such as substring search, longest common substring, and pattern matching. For example, to find all occurrences of a pattern P in a text T, we can construct the suffix array or suffix tree of T and then search for P in the suffix array or tree using binary search. The starting position of each match can be obtained from the corresponding entry in the suffix array or by traversing the path in the suffix tree corresponding to P. This approach has a time complexity of O(m log n) for a pattern of length m and a text of length n.

Another example is the construction of a Burrows-Wheeler transform (BWT) of a string, which is used in data compression and bioinformatics. The BWT of a string is a permutation of its characters that preserves the order of the substrings starting at each position. The suffix array or suffix tree can be used to efficiently compute the BWT of a string in O(n) time.

In summary, suffix arrays and suffix trees are powerful data structures that enable efficient processing of suffixes of a string and are useful in various string-related problems.

4.18 Explain the concept of a Least Recently Used (LRU) cache and how it can be implemented using data structures like a hash table and a doubly-linked list.

A Least Recently Used (LRU) cache is a type of cache that keeps track of the most recently accessed items. It has a maximum capacity and if this capacity is exceeded, it removes the least recently used item from the cache to make room for the new item. The LRU cache is commonly used in computer systems and software to optimize the use of memory.

To implement an LRU cache, two data structures are typically used: a hash table and a doubly-linked list. The hash table is used to store the key-value pairs, while the doubly-linked list is used to maintain the order of the items in the cache.

When an item is accessed in the cache, it is moved to the front of the doubly-linked list to indicate that it is the most recently used item. If the cache is at its maximum capacity and a new item needs to be added, the least recently used item from the end of the doubly-linked list is removed.

The time complexity of the LRU cache implementation is O(1) for both get and put operations when using a hash table and a doubly-linked list. The space complexity is O(n) since it requires space to store the key-value pairs in the hash table and the order of the items in the doubly-linked list.

Here is an example of an LRU cache implementation in Java:

```java
import java.util.HashMap;
import java.util.Map;

public class LRUCache {
    private Map<Integer, Node> map;
    private Node head;
    private Node tail;
    private int capacity;

    public LRUCache(int capacity) {
        this.map = new HashMap<>();
        this.head = null;
        this.tail = null;
        this.capacity = capacity;
    }

    public int get(int key) {
        Node node = map.get(key);
        if (node == null) {
            return -1;
        }
        // Move the node to the front of the list to indicate it is
            the most recently used item
        remove(node);
        setHead(node);
        return node.value;
    }

    public void put(int key, int value) {
        Node node = map.get(key);
        if (node == null) {
            node = new Node(key, value);
            map.put(key, node);
            if (map.size() > capacity) {
                // Remove the least recently used item from the end
                    of the list
                map.remove(tail.key);
                remove(tail);
            }
        } else {
            // Update the value of an existing node and move it to
                the front of the list
            node.value = value;
            remove(node);
        }
```

```
            setHead(node);
    }

    private void remove(Node node) {
        if (node.prev != null) {
            node.prev.next = node.next;
        } else {
            head = node.next;
        }
        if (node.next != null) {
            node.next.prev = node.prev;
        } else {
            tail = node.prev;
        }
    }

    private void setHead(Node node) {
        node.next = head;
        node.prev = null;
        if (head != null) {
            head.prev = node;
        }
        head = node;
        if (tail == null) {
            tail = head;
        }
    }

    private static class Node {
        private int key;
        private int value;
        private Node prev;
        private Node next;

        public Node(int key, int value) {
            this.key = key;
            this.value = value;
            this.prev = null;
            this.next = null;
        }
    }
}
```

4.19 Describe the difference between the Concurrency Control algorithms: Two-Phase Locking (2PL) and Timestamp Ordering (TO).

Concurrency control algorithms are used to ensure the consistency of a database system while multiple transactions are executed concurrently. Two common concurrency control algorithms are Two-

Phase Locking (2PL) and Timestamp Ordering (TO).

The Two-Phase Locking (2PL) algorithm is a locking-based concurrency control algorithm that operates in two phases: the growing phase and the shrinking phase. During the growing phase, a transaction acquires locks on all the data items it needs for its execution. Once a lock has been acquired, it cannot be released until the shrinking phase, which begins after the transaction has executed all its operations. During the shrinking phase, the transaction releases all its locks, allowing other transactions to access the data items. The 2PL algorithm ensures that a transaction's updates are serialized and that the database remains in a consistent state.

The Timestamp Ordering (TO) algorithm is a timestamp-based concurrency control algorithm that assigns a unique timestamp to each transaction that enters the system. The timestamp represents the order in which the transaction entered the system. When a transaction requests access to a data item, the system checks its timestamp against the timestamps of other transactions that have accessed the data item. If the requesting transaction has a higher timestamp than the other transactions, it is allowed to access the data item. Otherwise, the transaction is forced to wait until all transactions with lower timestamps have completed their operations. The TO algorithm ensures that transactions are executed in a serializable order, but it may result in more aborts and rollbacks compared to the 2PL algorithm.

In summary, the 2PL algorithm uses locks to ensure that transactions are executed serially and that the database remains in a consistent state, while the TO algorithm uses timestamps to enforce a serializable order of transactions. The choice of algorithm depends on the specific requirements of the system and the expected workload.

4.20 What is the Longest Increasing Subsequence problem, and how can it be solved using dynamic programming or other algorithmic approaches?

The Longest Increasing Subsequence (LIS) problem is the task of finding the length of the longest increasing subsequence of a given sequence of numbers. An increasing subsequence is a sequence of numbers in which each number is greater than the previous number. For example, in the sequence 3, 1, 4, 1, 5, 9, 2, 6, 5, the longest increasing subsequence is 1, 2, 5, 6 with length 4.

There are several algorithmic approaches to solving the LIS problem, including dynamic programming and binary search.

Dynamic programming is a common approach to solving the LIS problem. In this approach, we maintain a table that stores the length of the longest increasing subsequence ending at each element in the sequence. We start by initializing each element in the table to 1, since the longest increasing subsequence that ends at an element with only one number is itself. Then, for each element in the sequence, we compare it to all previous elements to see if it can be included in a longer increasing subsequence. If the element is greater than a previous element, we add 1 to the length of the longest increasing subsequence that ends at that previous element, and compare this length to the length of the longest increasing subsequence that ends at the current element. The length of the longest increasing subsequence that ends at the current element is then stored in the table.

Here is an example implementation of the dynamic programming approach to solving the LIS problem:

```
def lis(sequence):
    n = len(sequence)
    table = [1] * n
    for i in range(1, n):
        for j in range(i):
            if sequence[i] > sequence[j]:
                table[i] = max(table[i], table[j] + 1)
    return max(table)
```

The time complexity of this approach is $O(n^2)$, since we need to compare each element to all previous elements.

Another approach to solving the LIS problem is to use binary search. In this approach, we maintain a list of numbers that represent the smallest possible end element of an increasing subsequence of length i, for i=1,2,3,...,n. We start with an empty list, and for each element in the sequence, we perform a binary search on the list to find the index where the current element can be inserted to maintain the increasing order of the list. We then replace the element at that index with the current element, or append the current element to the list if it is greater than all elements in the list. The length of the list is the length of the longest increasing subsequence.

Here is an example implementation of the binary search approach to solving the LIS problem:

```
import bisect

def lis(sequence):
    n = len(sequence)
    ends = []
    for i in range(n):
        index = bisect.bisect_left(ends, sequence[i])
        if index == len(ends):
            ends.append(sequence[i])
        else:
            ends[index] = sequence[i]
    return len(ends)
```

The time complexity of this approach is $O(n \log n)$, since we perform a binary search for each element in the sequence.

Chapter 5

Expert

5.1 Explain the CAP theorem and its implications for distributed systems.

The CAP theorem is a concept used in distributed systems that defines the limitations of having three desirable properties in a distributed system: Consistency, Availability, and Partition tolerance. According to the theorem, it is impossible for a distributed system to provide all three properties simultaneously.

Consistency refers to the property of a system where all nodes see the same data at the same time. Availability refers to the property where a request to a node in a distributed system always results in a response, regardless of the state of the node or other nodes in the system. Partition tolerance refers to the property where a distributed system continues to function even if communication between nodes is lost or delayed.

The theorem states that in a distributed system, one can only have two of these properties at the same time. For example, if a system prioritizes consistency and partition tolerance, availability may suffer in case of network partitions. Similarly, if a system prioritizes availability and partition tolerance, consistency may suffer, as different nodes may have different versions of the data.

The implications of the CAP theorem in distributed systems are significant. It requires that designers of distributed systems prioritize the properties that are most critical to their use case, as they may not be able to achieve all three properties simultaneously. For instance, in a financial transaction system, consistency is the highest priority. Therefore, the designer may compromise availability in the event of network partitions. However, in a social media platform, availability may be a higher priority over consistency, meaning the system might not be entirely consistent, but it will always be available for users.

In summary, the CAP theorem has become an essential consideration in designing distributed systems, and understanding its implications is critical for designing effective and robust distributed systems.

5.2 Can you describe the consistent hashing technique and its applications in load balancing and distributed systems?

Consistent hashing is a technique that is used to partition data among a set of servers in a distributed system, with the goal of providing load balancing and fault tolerance. The technique works by mapping keys to servers in a way that is deterministic and evenly distributed.

In a consistent hashing system, the key space is divided into a number of partitions, typically using a hash function. Each server is assigned to one or more partitions, and is responsible for storing the data associated with the keys in those partitions. When a client wants to store or retrieve data, it uses the same hash function to determine which partition the key belongs to, and then sends the request to the server responsible for that partition.

One of the benefits of consistent hashing is that it allows servers to be added or removed from the system without requiring a full rehashing of the data. When a server is added, its partitions are assigned to it by redistributing some of the partitions from other servers, while leaving the rest of the partitions untouched. When a server is removed, its partitions are similarly redistributed to the remaining servers.

Consistent hashing has a number of applications in distributed systems. One of the most common is load balancing, where it is used to distribute client requests among a set of servers. By mapping each request to a specific server, consistent hashing ensures that requests are evenly distributed across the servers, and that the load is balanced.

Consistent hashing is also useful for providing fault tolerance. Because each key is mapped to a specific server, it is possible to replicate the data for each key to multiple servers, so that if one server fails, the data can be retrieved from another server that stores a copy of the data.

Overall, consistent hashing is a powerful technique that can be used to provide load balancing, fault tolerance, and other benefits in distributed systems. It is widely used in many large-scale systems, including content delivery networks, databases, and web applications.

5.3 What are the main differences between a deterministic and a non- deterministic algorithm? Provide examples of each type.

Deterministic and non-deterministic algorithms are two fundamental categories of algorithms in computer science. Deterministic algorithms are those that produce the same output for a given input, whereas non-deterministic algorithms may produce different outputs for the same input depending on the context or randomization.

One example of a deterministic algorithm is the binary search algorithm. This algorithm searches for a value in a sorted array by repeatedly dividing the array in half and comparing the target value with the middle element. The algorithm is guaranteed to find the target value in logarithmic time, and it always produces the same output for the same input.

In contrast, an example of a non-deterministic algorithm is the Monte Carlo algorithm. This algorithm uses randomization to solve problems that are difficult to solve deterministically. One application of the Monte Carlo algorithm is in approximating the value of pi. By randomly generating points within a square and counting the number of points that fall within a circle inscribed within the square, the algorithm can estimate the value of pi.

Another example of a non-deterministic algorithm is the probabilistic algorithm. Probabilistic algorithms use a probabilistic decision-making process to arrive at the correct solution with high probability. The Las Vegas algorithm is a type of probabilistic algorithm that guarantees a correct output with high probability but does not guarantee a fixed running time.

Overall, deterministic algorithms are more straightforward and predictable, while non-deterministic algorithms are more flexible and powerful but require additional computational resources. The choice of which type of algorithm to use depends on the specific problem and requirements of the application.

5.4 Explain the Burrows-Wheeler Transform (BWT) and its application in data compression.

The Burrows-Wheeler Transform (BWT) is a reversible permutation of a string that reorders the characters in the string in a way that makes it more compressible. The BWT has applications in data compression, where it is often used in conjunction with other compression techniques, such as Huffman coding.

The BWT works by taking a string of characters and rearranging it so that it is more compressible. The rearrangement is achieved by constructing a matrix of all possible rotations of the string, with the original string at the top of the matrix. The rows of the matrix are then sorted lexicographically, and the last column of the sorted matrix is extracted. This last column is the BWT of the original string.

For example, consider the string "banana". The matrix of all possible rotations of the string would look like this:

```
banana
anana$
nana$b
ana$na
na$nan
a$nanb
$nanab
```

Sorting the rows lexicographically results in the following matrix:

```
$nanab
a$nanb
ana$na
anana$
na$nan
nana$b
banana
```

The last column of the sorted matrix is "bn$aaa". This is the BWT of the original string "banana".

To decompress the BWT, the original string can be reconstructed using the BWT and a special index called the Burrows-Wheeler Transform Backward Index (BWTBI). The BWTBI is constructed by sorting the characters of the BWT and recording the positions of the characters in the sorted string. This index can then be used to reconstruct the original string by iteratively inserting characters from the BWT into a new string based on the position of the characters in the BWTBI.

In summary, the Burrows-Wheeler Transform is a technique for reordering the characters in a string to make it more compressible. It has applications in data compression and can be used in conjunction with other compression techniques, such as Huffman coding.

5.5 Describe the concept of locality-sensitive hashing (LSH) and its applications in approximate nearest neighbor search.

Locality-sensitive hashing (LSH) is a technique that allows efficient approximate nearest neighbor search by mapping similar items to the same hash bucket. The idea behind LSH is to design a hash function that maximizes the probability of collision for similar items and minimizes it for dissimilar items. By doing so, we can significantly reduce the search space for nearest neighbor search.

LSH is particularly useful in high-dimensional spaces where exact nearest neighbor search can be computationally expensive. In such cases, we can use LSH to reduce the search space to a subset of the data points that are likely to contain the nearest neighbor. This can lead to significant speedup in many applications, such as image and text retrieval, recommendation systems, and clustering.

The basic idea of LSH is to transform the high-dimensional data into a lower-dimensional space using a hash function. The hash function maps each data point to a hash key or signature, which is a low-dimensional representation of the original data. Similar data points are mapped to the same hash key with high probability, while dissimilar points are mapped to different keys. The hash keys are stored in hash tables, which are used to perform approximate nearest neighbor search.

One common LSH technique is called random projection. Random projection involves projecting the high-dimensional data onto a random hyperplane and using the sign of the resulting projection as the hash key. The hash function can be defined as follows:

```
h(x) = sign(w . x + b)
```

where w is a random vector, b is a random offset, and . represents the dot product. By choosing the random vectors carefully, we can design a hash function that maximizes the probability of collision for similar items and minimizes it for dissimilar items.

Another LSH technique is called minhashing. Minhashing involves representing each data point as a set of hash values, where each hash value corresponds to the minimum value of a randomly chosen hash function applied to the data point. By comparing the sets of hash values, we can estimate the similarity between two data points. Minhashing is commonly used in applications such as document similarity search.

LSH is a powerful technique for approximate nearest neighbor search, but it has some limitations. The quality of the approximation depends on the choice of hash function and the number of hash tables used. In addition, LSH is most effective when the data has a clustered structure, and it may not work well for highly uniform or sparse data. Nevertheless, LSH has many practical applications and continues to be an active area of research in machine learning and data mining.

5.6 What are Fenwick trees (also known as Binary Indexed Trees), and how can they be used for efficient range query operations?

Fenwick trees, also known as Binary Indexed Trees (BIT), are a data structure used for efficient range query operations on an array of numbers. They are particularly useful for computing the prefix sum of an array, as well as performing efficient range updates and queries.

The idea behind the Fenwick tree is to represent the array in a binary tree-like structure, where each node in the tree represents the sum of a range of elements in the array. The tree is constructed such that the parent node's value is the sum of its children nodes. The leaf nodes in the tree correspond to the elements of the original array. The depth of the tree is logarithmic to the length of the original array, resulting in efficient range query operations.

The operations that can be performed on a Fenwick tree are:

Prefix Sum: This operation returns the sum of all elements in the array up to a given index i. To compute the prefix sum, we simply traverse the tree from the leaf node at index i up to the root node, summing the values of all the nodes along the way.

Update: This operation updates the value of a single element in the array. To update an element, we traverse the tree from the leaf node corresponding to the index of the element up to the root node, updating the values of all the nodes along the way.

Range Sum: This operation returns the sum of all elements in the array between two indices i and j (inclusive). To compute the range sum, we compute the prefix sum for both indices i and j, and then subtract the prefix sum of i-1 from the prefix sum of j. This can be done efficiently using the Fenwick tree.

Fenwick trees have a time complexity of O(log n) for both update and prefix sum operations, and O(log n) for range sum operations. They are particularly useful when there are many range query operations to be performed on the array, and the array is updated frequently. They are commonly used in image processing, computational geometry, and other areas of computer science where efficient range query operations are required.

5.7 Explain the difference between online and offline algorithms, providing examples of each.

Online and offline algorithms are two broad categories of algorithms that differ in the way they receive their input data.

Offline Algorithms

Offline algorithms, also known as batch algorithms, receive all their input data at once and process it to produce a final output. They assume that all data is available in advance and do not make any decisions until they have seen the entire input. These algorithms typically have high time and space complexity, since they operate on the entire data set at once. Some examples of offline algorithms include sorting algorithms like merge sort, quicksort, and heapsort.

Online Algorithms

Online algorithms, on the other hand, receive their input data in a sequential manner and must make decisions based on the data they have seen so far. These algorithms process the data in real-time, without knowing the entire data set in advance. Online algorithms have limited access to the input data, as they can only see the current and previous data elements. This often leads to suboptimal results compared to offline algorithms, but they can be more efficient and practical for large or continuously streaming data. Some examples of online algorithms include search algorithms like linear search, and algorithms for network routing and load balancing.

Differences

The key difference between online and offline algorithms is in the way they process input data. Offline algorithms have the advantage of seeing all data at once and can optimize their decisions based on the entire data set. This can lead to better performance in terms of time and space complexity, and more accurate results. However, offline algorithms may not be suitable for applications where data is not available in advance, or where the input data is too large to process at once. In contrast, online algorithms can handle data as it arrives and can make decisions in real-time, making them more suitable for streaming and time-sensitive applications. However, online algorithms may not provide the same level of accuracy or performance as offline algorithms, since they make decisions based only on partial information.

In general, the choice of online or offline algorithm depends on the specific application and the characteristics of the input data. For applications where data is continuously streaming and time-sensitive, online algorithms may be more suitable. For applications where data is available in advance and can be processed in bulk, offline algorithms may be more appropriate.

5.8 Describe the concept of spectral graph theory and its applications in data analysis and machine learning.

Spectral graph theory is a field of mathematics that studies the relationship between the properties of a graph and the eigenvalues and eigenvectors of its adjacency matrix or Laplacian matrix. It provides a powerful set of tools for analyzing complex networks and understanding their structural properties, as well as for developing machine learning algorithms that operate on graph data.

The adjacency matrix of a graph is a square matrix that represents the graph by indicating which vertices are adjacent to each other. If the graph has N vertices, the adjacency matrix is an N x N matrix A, where the entry A[i][j] is 1 if there is an edge from vertex i to vertex j, and 0 otherwise. The Laplacian matrix of a graph is defined as $L = D - A$, where D is a diagonal matrix that contains the degree of each vertex on its diagonal.

One of the main applications of spectral graph theory is in clustering, where the goal is to partition the vertices of a graph into groups or communities based on their connectivity patterns. This can be done by finding the eigenvectors of the Laplacian matrix, which provide a natural embedding of the graph into a high-dimensional Euclidean space. The spectral clustering algorithm works by first computing the k smallest eigenvectors of the Laplacian matrix, and then using them as features for clustering using techniques like k-means or hierarchical clustering.

Another application of spectral graph theory is in graph drawing and visualization, where the goal is to represent a graph in a way that reveals its underlying structure and relationships. Spectral graph drawing algorithms use the eigenvectors of the Laplacian matrix to map the vertices of the graph onto a low-dimensional space, where they can be visualized using techniques like force-directed layout or multidimensional scaling.

Spectral graph theory also has applications in machine learning, particularly in the field of graph neural networks. Graph neural networks are a class of deep learning models that operate on graph data, and spectral graph theory provides a foundation for understanding their behavior and performance. For example, the graph convolutional neural network (GCN) model uses the eigenvectors of the Laplacian matrix to define a graph convolution operation, which enables the network to learn features that capture the local and global structure of the graph.

In summary, spectral graph theory is a powerful framework for analyzing and understanding the structure of complex networks, and it has important applications in clustering, graph drawing, and machine learning.

5.9 Explain the various strategies for handling collisions in hash tables, such as linear probing, quadratic probing, and double hashing.

A hash table is a data structure that stores elements using a hash function to map keys to indices of an array. However, two different keys may map to the same index, leading to a collision. There are various strategies for handling collisions in hash tables, such as linear probing, quadratic probing, and double hashing.

Linear probing: In linear probing, when a collision occurs, the algorithm checks the next available slot in the array sequentially until an empty slot is found. The new key is then inserted into that slot. For example, suppose we have a hash table with the following indices: [A, B, C, D, E]. If a new key maps to index B, and B is already occupied, the algorithm will check index C, then D, and so on, until an empty slot is found.

Quadratic probing: Quadratic probing uses a similar approach to linear probing but checks the array indices using a quadratic function. For example, if a collision occurs at index B, the algorithm checks the next available slots using the function $(i + 1^2), (i + 2^2), (i + 3^2)$, and so on.

Double hashing: Double hashing uses two hash functions to compute the index of the array where the new key should be inserted. If a collision occurs, the algorithm applies the second hash function to the key and checks the next available slot in the array. The double hashing technique aims to reduce the likelihood of collisions.

Each strategy has its advantages and disadvantages. Linear probing can result in clustering, where groups of elements occupy contiguous slots in the array. Quadratic probing can cause secondary clustering, where elements tend to cluster around the same locations. Double hashing can provide better distribution of elements in the array but requires two hash functions.

In general, the choice of collision resolution strategy depends on the characteristics of the data and the performance requirements of the application.

5.10 What are the main techniques for parallelizing algorithms, and how can they improve the performance of computation-intensive tasks?

Parallel computing is a technique of dividing a large computation task into smaller sub-tasks that can be executed simultaneously on different processors or cores. Parallelizing algorithms can improve the performance of computation-intensive tasks by reducing the time taken to execute them. There are several techniques for parallelizing algorithms, and some of the main ones are:

Data Parallelism: This technique involves dividing the input data into smaller chunks and assigning them to different processors or cores for parallel processing. This is useful when the computation can be easily broken down into independent sub-tasks that operate on different data elements.

For example, suppose we have to calculate the sum of a large array of numbers. In this case, we can divide the array into smaller chunks and assign them to different processors for parallel computation. Once the computations are complete, we can combine the results from each processor to get the final output.

Task Parallelism: This technique involves dividing the computation task into smaller sub-tasks that can be executed independently on different processors or cores. Task parallelism is useful when the computation can be broken down into smaller, interdependent sub-tasks.

For example, suppose we have to process a large number of images, each of which involves several sub-tasks such as image preprocessing, feature extraction, and classification. In this case, we can divide the processing of each image into smaller sub-tasks and assign them to different processors for parallel processing. Once the sub-tasks are complete, we can combine the results to get the final output.

Pipelining: This technique involves dividing the computation task into a series of stages, with each stage performing a specific computation on the input data. The output of each stage is passed as input to the next stage, and the stages operate in parallel on different parts of the input data.

For example, suppose we have to perform image processing on a large number of images. In this case, we can divide the processing into a series of stages such as image pre-processing, feature extraction, and classification. Each stage can operate on different parts of the input data, and the output of each stage is passed to the next stage. This technique can improve the overall performance of the computation by overlapping the computation of different stages.

SIMD (Single Instruction, Multiple Data) Parallelism: This technique involves executing the same instruction on multiple data elements simultaneously. SIMD parallelism is useful when the same operation needs to be performed on a large number of data elements.

For example, suppose we have to calculate the sum of two large arrays. In this case, we can use SIMD parallelism to add the corresponding elements of the two arrays simultaneously, improving the overall performance of the computation.

In conclusion, parallelizing algorithms can significantly improve the performance of computation-intensive tasks. The choice of parallelization technique depends on the nature of the computation and the type of data being processed. By using a suitable parallelization technique, we can reduce the time taken to perform complex computations, making them more efficient and scalable.

5.11 Describe the concept of an external merge sort and its applications in handling large datasets that do not fit in memory.

External merge sort is an algorithm used to sort large datasets that do not fit into memory. It is designed for situations where the amount of data to be sorted is too large to fit in the main memory of a computer. External merge sort is commonly used for sorting large files, such as log files, database tables, or scientific data sets. The algorithm is based on the merge sort algorithm, but it is adapted to work with files instead of arrays.

The external merge sort algorithm works by dividing the input data into smaller chunks that can be sorted in memory, and then merging these chunks into larger and larger sorted chunks until the entire dataset is sorted. The basic steps of the algorithm are as follows:

Divide the input data into smaller chunks, called runs, that can fit into memory. Sort each run using an internal sorting algorithm, such as quicksort or heapsort. Merge the sorted runs into larger sorted chunks using a merging algorithm, such as a k-way merge algorithm. Repeat steps 2 and 3 until the entire dataset is sorted.

The key idea behind external merge sort is to minimize the number of disk accesses required to sort the data. The algorithm achieves this by minimizing the amount of data that needs to be read from and written to disk during each pass of the sorting process.

One of the key challenges of external merge sort is choosing an appropriate block size for the runs. If the block size is too small, then the algorithm will spend too much time reading and writing data to disk. If the block size is too large, then the algorithm will not be able to fit all the runs into memory at once, which will slow down the sorting process.

Overall, external merge sort is an effective algorithm for sorting large datasets that do not fit into memory. It is widely used in applications such as database management systems, scientific data processing, and log file analysis.

5.12 Explain the difference between global and local alignment in sequence alignment algorithms, and provide examples of algorithms for each.

Sequence alignment algorithms are a fundamental component of computational biology and bioinformatics. They are used to compare and find similarities between DNA, RNA, or protein sequences. The alignment process involves assigning scores to all possible alignments of two sequences and then finding the alignment(s) with the highest score. There are two main types of sequence alignment: global and local alignment.

Global alignment is used to compare two entire sequences and identify the best overall alignment between them. It aims to align as many characters as possible, even if some mismatches or gaps are necessary. The Needleman-Wunsch algorithm is a classic example of a global alignment algorithm. It uses dynamic programming to find the optimal alignment between two sequences by constructing a matrix of scores and then backtracking through the matrix to find the optimal path. The resulting alignment shows the similarities and differences between the two sequences across their entire length.

Local alignment, on the other hand, is used to identify regions of similarity between two sequences. It aims to find the best alignment between two subsequences within the two sequences, even if the rest of the sequences do not align well. The Smith-Waterman algorithm is a classic example of a local alignment algorithm. It also uses dynamic programming to find the optimal alignment, but instead of aligning the entire sequences, it only aligns a subset of the sequences that produce the highest score.

The difference between global and local alignment is best illustrated with an example. Consider the following two DNA sequences:

- Sequence 1: AGCTGTTACGAGTCGT
- Sequence 2: GCTGATTACAGTCGTA

A global alignment of these two sequences might result in:

- Sequence 1: AGCTGTTACGAGTCGT-
- Sequence 2: -GCTGATTACAGTCGTA

This alignment shows the best overall alignment between the two sequences. The "-" represents a gap inserted to align the two sequences. However, this alignment ignores the fact that there is a highly similar region between the two sequences:

- Sequence 1: AGCTGTTACGAGTCGT
- Sequence 2: GCTGATTACAGTCGTA

A local alignment of these two sequences would identify this highly similar region:

- Sequence 1: TGTTACGA
- Sequence 2: TTA-CAGT

This alignment shows the best alignment between the two subsequences that produces the highest score. The "-" represents a gap inserted to align the two sequences.

In summary, global alignment aims to align the entire sequences and identify the best overall alignment, while local alignment focuses on identifying regions of similarity between the two sequences, even if the rest of the sequences do not align well.

5.13 What is the Maximum Flow problem, and how do the Ford-Fulkerson and Edmonds-Karp algorithms solve it?

The Maximum Flow problem is a classic problem in computer science and graph theory, which involves determining the maximum amount of flow that can be sent from a source node to a sink node in a flow network.

A flow network is a directed graph where each edge has a capacity, representing the maximum amount of flow that can be sent through that edge. The goal is to find the maximum flow from the source node to the sink node, subject to the capacity constraints.

The Ford-Fulkerson algorithm is an algorithm for solving the Maximum Flow problem. The basic idea is to start with an initial feasible flow and repeatedly augment the flow until no more flow can be sent from the source to the sink. The algorithm finds a path from the source to the sink in the residual graph, which is the graph that results from subtracting the current flow from the capacity of each edge. If a path exists, the algorithm finds the minimum capacity edge along the path, adds that capacity to the flow, and updates the residual graph accordingly. The algorithm repeats until no more paths can be found in the residual graph.

While the Ford-Fulkerson algorithm is correct, it can take a long time to converge, and the worst-case running time is not well-defined. The Edmonds-Karp algorithm is a variation of the Ford-Fulkerson algorithm that uses a BFS (breadth-first search) to find the shortest path in the residual graph from the source to the sink. This ensures that the algorithm always terminates in $O(E^2V)$ time, where E is the number of edges and V is the number of vertices in the graph.

In summary, the Maximum Flow problem is a fundamental problem in graph theory, and the Ford-Fulkerson and Edmonds-Karp algorithms are widely used for solving it. These algorithms have many practical applications, including in transportation planning, network optimization, and resource allocation.

5.14 Describe the concept of Monte Carlo algorithms and provide an example of a problem that can be solved using this technique.

Monte Carlo algorithms are a class of randomized algorithms that use random sampling to solve problems that may be deterministic but are too complex to solve using traditional methods. These algorithms provide an approximate solution to the problem by simulating a large number of possible outcomes and analyzing their statistical properties.

One classic example of a problem that can be solved using Monte Carlo algorithms is estimating the value of . The algorithm involves generating random points within a square and checking whether they fall within a quarter of a circle inscribed in the square. The ratio of the number of points within the circle to the total number of points generated approaches /4 as the number of points generated approaches infinity.

Another example is the Monte Carlo tree search (MCTS) algorithm, which is used in game AI to make decisions based on statistical simulations. MCTS simulates a large number of possible moves from the current game state and evaluates their potential outcomes using a scoring function. The algorithm selects the move with the highest expected outcome, taking into account the randomness of the simulations.

Monte Carlo algorithms have wide applications in various fields, including finance, physics, engineering, and computer science. However, their accuracy and efficiency depend on the quality and number of the generated random samples. Therefore, careful analysis and tuning are required to ensure the correctness and performance of these algorithms.

5.15 Explain the Fast Fourier Transform (FFT) algorithm and its applications in signal processing and other computational tasks.

The Fast Fourier Transform (FFT) is an efficient algorithm for calculating the discrete Fourier transform (DFT) of a sequence, which is an important operation in many fields, including signal processing, data analysis, and scientific computing. The FFT reduces the time complexity of computing the DFT from $O(n^2)$ to $O(nlogn)$, making it feasible to process large data sets.

The basic idea behind the FFT is to exploit the properties of complex roots of unity to divide a DFT of size N into two smaller DFTs of size N/2, and then recursively compute the DFTs of these smaller sequences. The FFT can be implemented using either a divide-and-conquer approach or a radix-2 algorithm.

In practice, the FFT is used in a wide range of applications, such as audio and video processing, image analysis, wireless communication, and scientific simulations. For example, in audio processing, the FFT can be used to transform a time-domain signal into its frequency-domain representation, allowing for the identification of specific frequencies and patterns in the signal. Similarly, in image analysis, the FFT can be used for tasks such as edge detection, image enhancement, and feature extraction.

Overall, the FFT is a powerful tool for processing large amounts of data efficiently and accurately, making it an essential component of many computational tasks.

5.16 What is the difference between eager and lazy data structures? Provide examples of each type.

Eager and lazy data structures are two different approaches to handling data manipulation and computation. The primary difference between the two is when the computation is performed.

Eager data structures, also known as strict data structures, compute their results immediately upon receiving input. This means that whenever a value is added or modified in the data structure, any relevant computations are performed right away. Eager data structures are useful when the amount of data is small, and there are no significant computational overheads to worry about.

Examples of eager data structures include arrays, linked lists, and binary search trees. When an element is added to an array, for instance, the size of the array increases immediately, and the new value is assigned to the appropriate index.

Lazy data structures, also known as non-strict data structures, defer computations until the results are needed. This approach is useful when the computation is expensive, and it is not necessary to compute all possible results upfront. Lazy data structures can be more efficient than eager data structures when dealing with large amounts of data because the computations are only performed when needed.

Examples of lazy data structures include lazy evaluation in functional programming, and lazy propagation in segment trees. In functional programming, expressions are not evaluated immediately but are instead stored as unevaluated thunks that are evaluated only when their results are needed. In segment trees, lazy propagation is used to defer updates to the tree until they are necessary, thus reducing the number of updates that need to be performed.

In summary, the choice between eager and lazy data structures depends on the specific requirements of the problem at hand. Eager data structures are useful when the data is small, and the computations are inexpensive, while lazy data structures are more efficient when dealing with large amounts of data and expensive computations.

5.17 Describe the concept of space-filling curves and their applications in multi-dimensional data indexing.

Space-filling curves are a class of curves that traverse a multi-dimensional space in a way that covers as much area as possible with a single continuous line. They are widely used in multi-dimensional data indexing and retrieval systems to map multi-dimensional data to one dimension, which makes it easier to store and search.

One of the most famous space-filling curves is the Hilbert curve, which is a continuous and self-similar curve that fills a square. The curve can be used to map points in a two-dimensional space to a one-dimensional line, which makes it easier to store and retrieve them. The mapping is done by dividing the square into smaller squares recursively and assigning a binary code to each square based on its position within the larger square. The binary codes of the squares are then concatenated to form a one-dimensional code that represents the entire curve.

The Hilbert curve can be extended to higher dimensions, and other space-filling curves have been developed for higher dimensions as well, such as the Peano curve and the Z-order curve. These curves have similar properties to the Hilbert curve, and can also be used to map multi-dimensional data to a one-dimensional line.

Space-filling curves are used in a variety of applications, such as database indexing, image compression, and scientific simulations. In database indexing, space-filling curves are used to map multi-dimensional data to a one-dimensional index, which makes it faster to search and retrieve data. In image compression, space-filling curves can be used to compress images by representing the pixels along the curve, which reduces the amount of data that needs to be stored. In scientific simulations, space-filling curves can be used to map multi-dimensional data to a one-dimensional line, which makes it easier to analyze and visualize the data.

5.18 Explain the various algorithms used for garbage collection in programming languages, such as mark-and-sweep, reference counting, and generational garbage collection.

Garbage collection is an essential technique used by programming languages to automatically reclaim memory that is no longer needed by the program. In this process, the garbage collector identifies objects that are no longer reachable by the program and frees the memory used by those objects.

There are different algorithms for garbage collection, each with its advantages and disadvantages. Here are some of the most common algorithms:

Mark-and-sweep: This is one of the simplest garbage collection algorithms. It works by first marking all objects that are reachable from the root set (e.g., the stack and global variables). It then sweeps through the entire heap, freeing the memory used by any unmarked objects. The disadvantage of this algorithm is that it can suffer from fragmentation, which can result in memory fragmentation and slow down the program.

Reference counting: This algorithm works by keeping track of the number of references to each object. Whenever an object is no longer referenced, its memory can be reclaimed. The advantage of this algorithm is that it can reclaim memory as soon as an object becomes unreachable, without waiting for a garbage collection cycle. However, it suffers from the problem of circular references, where two or more objects reference each other and thus cannot be garbage collected even if they are unreachable.

Generational garbage collection: This algorithm takes advantage of the fact that most objects have a short lifespan and are only used for a short period of time. It divides the heap into multiple generations, with younger generations containing recently created objects, and older generations containing long-lived objects. Garbage collection is performed more frequently on younger generations, while older generations are collected less often. This approach can reduce the overall cost of garbage collection, but it requires more complex algorithms to manage the different generations.

There are other algorithms for garbage collection, such as copying collection, mark-sweep-compact, and tri-color marking. Each algorithm has its strengths and weaknesses, and the choice of algorithm depends on factors such as the programming language, the type of application, and the memory requirements of the program.

In general, garbage collection algorithms play a crucial role in modern programming languages, as they enable developers to write code that is more efficient and less error-prone. However, they also introduce some overhead and can sometimes make the program less predictable in terms of memory usage and performance.

5.19 What is the stable marriage problem, and how can it be solved using the Gale-Shapley algorithm?

The stable marriage problem is a classic problem in mathematics and computer science that deals with finding a stable matching between two sets of people with different preferences. In this problem, there are n men and n women, and each person has a list of preferences ranking the members of the opposite sex from best to worst.

The goal is to match the men and women in such a way that there are no "rogue" pairs who would prefer to be with each other than with their assigned partner. In other words, the matching should be stable, meaning that there should be no two pairs (man-woman) who prefer each other to their assigned partners.

The Gale-Shapley algorithm, also known as the Deferred Acceptance algorithm, is a popular algorithm for solving the stable marriage problem. It works by having each man propose to the woman he most prefers who has not yet rejected him, and the women then choose the best proposal among those they have received so far. If a woman rejects a proposal, she cannot receive any more proposals from that man, but if she accepts a proposal, she is provisionally matched with that man.

The algorithm then continues with the men proposing to the women they most prefer among those who have not rejected them, and the women choosing the best proposal among those they have received so far. This process continues until every woman is provisionally matched with a man.

The Gale-Shapley algorithm guarantees that the matching it produces is stable, meaning that there is no pair of people who would both prefer to be with each other than with their current partner. Moreover, the algorithm produces a matching that is optimal for the proposing side, meaning that no man can be matched with a woman he prefers less than the one he is matched with.

The time complexity of the Gale-Shapley algorithm is $O(n^2)$, where n is the number of men and women. This makes the algorithm relatively efficient, even for large datasets.

Example: Suppose there are three men (M1, M2, M3) and three women (W1, W2, W3), and their preference lists are as follows:

```
M1: W1 > W2 > W3
M2: W2 > W1 > W3
M3: W3 > W2 > W1

W1: M2 > M3 > M1
W2: M1 > M3 > M2
W3: M2 > M1 > M3
```

The algorithm proceeds as follows:

- M1 proposes to W1, who accepts provisionally.

- M2 proposes to W1, who rejects him.

- M2 proposes to W2, who accepts provisionally.

- M3 proposes to W3, who accepts provisionally.

- M1 proposes to W2, who rejects him.

- M1 proposes to W3, who accepts provisionally.

The resulting stable matching is as follows:

- M1 is matched with W3

- M2 is matched with W2

- M3 is matched with W1

This matching is stable because there is no pair of people who would both prefer to be with each other than with their current partner.

5.20 Describe the concept of a concurrent data structure and discuss the challenges in designing and implementing them for multi-threaded applications. Provide an example of a widely-used concurrent data structure.

A concurrent data structure is a data structure that can be accessed and modified simultaneously by multiple threads or processes, without causing inconsistencies or data races. In a multi-threaded environment, concurrent data structures are critical to ensure safe and efficient data sharing and synchronization between threads.

Designing and implementing concurrent data structures is challenging because they require careful consideration of thread-safety, synchronization, and performance. In particular, concurrent data structures must ensure that no two threads can modify the structure at the same time, as this can lead to inconsistencies and data races. Additionally, they should provide efficient and scalable access to data, as contention between threads can result in performance degradation and thread starvation.

One widely-used concurrent data structure is the Concurrent Hash Map, which is a hash table that supports concurrent access and modifications by multiple threads. The Concurrent Hash Map uses a technique called lock striping, which divides the hash table into multiple segments or buckets, each protected by a separate lock. This allows multiple threads to access different segments concurrently, without blocking each other. When a thread wants to access a particular element in the hash table, it acquires the lock for the corresponding segment and performs the operation. If multiple threads access the same segment concurrently, they must contend for the lock, but the contention is limited to that segment only, reducing the overall contention and improving performance.

Another important concurrent data structure is the Concurrent Queue, which is a queue that supports concurrent insertions and removals by multiple threads. The Concurrent Queue uses lock-free algorithms, such as Compare-and-Swap (CAS), to perform atomic updates to the queue's head and tail pointers. When a thread wants to enqueue an item, it creates a new node and attempts to atomically update the tail pointer using CAS. If another thread enqueues an item concurrently, the CAS operation fails, and the thread retries the operation. When a thread wants to dequeue an item, it atomically updates the head pointer and removes the first node from the queue. If another thread dequeues an item concurrently, the head pointer is updated by that thread, and the other thread retries the operation.

Overall, concurrent data structures are critical for developing efficient and scalable multi-threaded applications. They provide safe and synchronized access to data, while minimizing contention and ensuring high performance.

Chapter 6

Guru

6.1 Explain the concept of algorithmic information theory and its relation to Kolmogorov complexity.

Algorithmic information theory is a field that studies the amount of information contained in an object, particularly in an algorithmic sense. It is concerned with the amount of information required to represent or describe an object, and how efficiently it can be compressed. The central idea is that the amount of information in an object is related to the length of the shortest program that can produce it.

Kolmogorov complexity is a measure of the information content of an object based on the length of the shortest program that can produce it. The Kolmogorov complexity of an object is the length of the shortest binary program that produces the object when executed on a universal Turing machine. This measure is uncomputable in general, since it requires a universal algorithm that can compute the shortest program for any given object.

Despite its theoretical limitations, algorithmic information theory has many practical applications, particularly in data compression and machine learning. In data compression, the goal is to find the shortest representation of a data set that preserves its information content. In machine learning, the goal is to find the simplest model that accurately captures the patterns in a data set.

One of the most famous examples of algorithmic information theory is the concept of the "incompressibility method". This method is used to prove that certain problems are unsolvable by reducing them to the problem of determining the Kolmogorov complexity of a given string. For example, the halting problem, which asks whether a given program will eventually halt or run forever, can be reduced to the problem of determining the Kolmogorov complexity of a particular string.

In summary, algorithmic information theory provides a mathematical framework for studying the information content of objects and the efficiency of algorithms for representing and processing them. It has many practical applications in fields such as data compression, machine learning, and cryptography, and has led to important insights into the nature of computation and the limits of our ability to reason about complex systems.

6.2   Describe the concept of NP-completeness and its implications for the tractability of problems.

NP-completeness is a concept in computational complexity theory that deals with the classification of problems based on their computational complexity. NP stands for "nondeterministic polynomial time," which refers to the class of decision problems that can be solved by a nondeterministic Turing machine in polynomial time. NP-completeness is a property of decision problems, which are problems that have a yes or no answer.

A problem is said to be NP-complete if it is in the class NP and every other problem in NP can be reduced to it in polynomial time. This means that if we can solve an NP-complete problem in polynomial time, then we can solve all other problems in NP in polynomial time as well. However, no polynomial-time algorithm is currently known for solving NP-complete problems, which makes them some of the most difficult problems in computer science.

NP-complete problems have many practical applications, including scheduling, optimization, logistics, and cryptography. Some examples of NP-complete problems include the traveling salesman problem, the knapsack problem, the vertex cover problem, and the Boolean satisfiability problem.

The difficulty of NP-complete problems has important implications for the design and analysis of algorithms. In practice, many real-world problems are NP-complete, and so algorithms that solve these problems exactly are typically not practical for large instances. Instead, approximate algorithms or heuristics are often used to find good solutions quickly, even though they may not be optimal.

In summary, NP-completeness is a fundamental concept in computational complexity theory that identifies a class of problems that are some of the most difficult to solve in computer science. The fact that many real-world problems are NP-complete underscores the importance of developing efficient algorithms for approximate or heuristic solutions.

6.3 Discuss the different types of approximation algorithms, such as polynomial-time approximation schemes (PTAS), and provide an example of a problem that can be solved using these techniques.

Approximation algorithms are techniques used in computer science to solve computationally difficult problems when an exact solution is infeasible to find within a reasonable amount of time. The aim is to find an approximate solution that is close enough to the optimal solution, ideally with a known degree of accuracy.

There are several types of approximation algorithms, including:

Polynomial-time approximation schemes (PTAS): These algorithms are designed to give a solution that is within a specified factor of the optimal solution, and the time complexity is a polynomial function of the input size and the approximation factor. A classic example of a problem that can be solved using a PTAS is the Knapsack problem, where the goal is to select a subset of items with maximum value that fits within a given capacity.

Fully polynomial-time approximation schemes (FPTAS): These algorithms are similar to PTAS but are more efficient in terms of time complexity, as the polynomial function depends on both the input size and the desired precision. The most well-known example of an FPTAS is the Dynamic Time Warping problem, where the goal is to find the optimal alignment between two time series with minimum distance.

Randomized approximation algorithms: These algorithms use randomness to quickly find an approximate solution that is close to the optimal solution with high probability. The quality of the solution can be improved by running the algorithm multiple times. An example of a problem that can be solved using a randomized algorithm is the Max-Cut problem, where the goal is to partition the nodes of a graph into two sets with maximum number of edges between them.

Greedy approximation algorithms: These algorithms make locally optimal choices at each step in the hope of finding a globally optimal solution. They are usually fast and easy to implement, but may not always produce the best possible approximation. An example of a problem that can be solved using a greedy algorithm is the Set Cover problem, where the goal is to select a minimum number of sets that cover all elements of a given universe.

In general, approximation algorithms are useful for solving many real-world problems where finding an exact solution is impractical or even impossible. They can provide reasonably good solutions quickly, even for large-scale problems, and can be a useful tool for decision-making in fields such as finance, logistics, and engineering.

6.4 Explain the concept of randomized algorithms and their applications in solving computational problems. Provide an example of a widely-used randomized algorithm.

Randomized algorithms are those that use a random element to solve a problem. These algorithms use randomness to generate a solution to a problem that is correct with high probability, rather than being completely deterministic. Randomized algorithms are useful in solving problems for which no deterministic algorithm exists or for which deterministic algorithms are computationally infeasible.

One example of a widely-used randomized algorithm is the Quick-Sort algorithm, which is used for sorting a list of elements. Quick-Sort selects a random element from the list, called the pivot, and partitions the remaining elements into two groups based on whether they are greater than or less than the pivot. This process is repeated recursively on each group until the entire list is sorted.

Another example is the Monte Carlo algorithm for estimating the value of pi. This algorithm uses random sampling to estimate the value of pi by generating random points within a square and counting the number of points that fall within a quarter circle inscribed in the square. The ratio of the number of points within the quarter circle to the total number of points sampled can be used to estimate the value of pi.

Randomized algorithms are also used in cryptography, where they provide a level of security by making it difficult to predict the output of an algorithm even with knowledge of the input. One example of such an algorithm is the RSA algorithm, which is used for secure communication over the internet. The RSA algorithm relies on the difficulty of factoring large prime numbers, which is a computationally difficult problem.

In general, randomized algorithms are used when a deterministic algorithm would be too slow or impractical, or when a probabilistic solution is acceptable. However, randomized algorithms also have some drawbacks, including the possibility of generating incorrect results, the difficulty of analyzing their worst-case performance, and the need to generate random numbers efficiently.

6.5 Discuss the role of data structures and algorithms in modern cryptography, specifically in relation to symmetric and asymmetric encryption.

Data structures and algorithms play a crucial role in modern cryptography by providing efficient and secure ways of storing and processing sensitive information. In this context, symmetric and asymmetric encryption are two important cryptographic techniques that use different data structures and algorithms.

Symmetric encryption is a technique where the same secret key is used for both encryption and decryption of data. This technique uses data structures such as hash tables, binary trees, and arrays, and algorithms such as the Advanced Encryption Standard (AES) and the Data Encryption Standard (DES). These algorithms rely on efficient data structures and algorithms to perform key management, encryption, and decryption operations quickly and securely.

Asymmetric encryption, on the other hand, is a technique where two different keys are used for encryption and decryption. This technique uses data structures such as public-key cryptography and digital signatures, and algorithms such as the Rivest-Shamir-Adleman (RSA) algorithm and the Elliptic Curve Cryptography (ECC) algorithm. These algorithms rely on sophisticated data structures and algorithms to securely manage and exchange keys, encrypt and decrypt data, and verify digital signatures.

In addition to encryption techniques, data structures and algorithms also play an important role in cryptographic protocols such as secure hash functions, digital certificates, and secure communication protocols. Hash functions, for example, are used to generate unique and secure representations of data, while digital certificates are used to verify the identity of users and devices in a secure way. Communication protocols such as Transport Layer Security (TLS) and Secure Sockets Layer (SSL) rely on complex data structures and algorithms to establish secure connections between clients and servers.

Overall, data structures and algorithms are critical components of modern cryptography, providing efficient and secure ways of storing, processing, and transmitting sensitive information. The use of these techniques ensures the confidentiality, integrity, and availability of data, protecting users and organizations from security threats and attacks.

6.6   Describe the concept of succinct data structures and their applications in space-efficient representation of large datasets.

Succinct data structures are a class of space-efficient data structures that can represent large amounts of data using a minimal amount of space, while still allowing for efficient querying and manipulation. They achieve this by exploiting the redundancy and structure present in the data being represented.

Succinct data structures are particularly useful when dealing with massive datasets, where the amount of storage required to represent the data becomes a limiting factor. Examples of such datasets include genomic data, social network graphs, and web page repositories. In these cases, succinct data structures allow for the efficient storage and processing of data while still maintaining the ability to perform complex queries and analyses.

One common example of a succinct data structure is the compressed suffix array, which is used for efficient text indexing and search. The compressed suffix array represents the suffixes of a text string in sorted order, using a combination of suffix sorting and compression techniques. This structure allows for fast substring queries, as well as a variety of other text-related operations.

Another example of a succinct data structure is the wavelet tree, which is used for efficient range querying on large sets of integers.

The wavelet tree recursively divides the input set into two smaller subsets, and then stores information about the partitioning at each level of recursion. This allows for efficient range queries, as well as a variety of other operations such as rank and select.

Succinct data structures also play an important role in the design of data compression algorithms. By representing the data in a compressed form, these structures allow for more efficient storage and transmission of data. One example of a compression algorithm that uses succinct data structures is the Burrows-Wheeler transform, which is used as a preprocessing step in many popular compression algorithms such as bzip2 and gzip.

Overall, succinct data structures are a powerful tool in the design and analysis of large-scale data systems. By providing efficient and space-efficient representations of large datasets, these structures allow for faster and more effective processing of data, enabling a wide range of applications in fields such as genomics, web search, and machine learning.

6.7 Explain the principle of duality in computational geometry and its applications in solving geometric problems.

The principle of duality in computational geometry is a fundamental concept that relates geometric objects to their dual counterparts. It states that for any property or theorem that holds for a given geometric object, there is a dual property or theorem that holds for the dual object. In other words, the dual of a geometric object is obtained by interchanging points and lines, or hyperplanes and halfspaces, in a given space.

The concept of duality can be applied to a wide range of geometric problems, such as convex hulls, Voronoi diagrams, Delaunay triangulations, and arrangement of lines. For example, the duality between the convex hull and Voronoi diagram of a set of points in the plane is a well-known result in computational geometry. The convex hull of a set of points is the smallest convex polygon that contains all the points, while the Voronoi diagram of the points is a partition of the plane into regions, where each region corresponds to a point and contains all the points that are closer to it than to any other point.

The dual relationship between the convex hull and Voronoi diagram is established by the following properties: The vertex of the Voronoi diagram corresponds to an edge of the convex hull, and the edge of the Voronoi diagram corresponds to a vertex of the convex hull. Moreover, the dual of a convex polygon is a Voronoi diagram, and the dual of a Voronoi diagram is a convex polyhedron.

The duality principle also plays an important role in algorithm design and analysis in computational geometry. For example, the dual of an algorithm for solving a geometric problem can be used to solve a dual problem, which often leads to new insights and solutions. Duality can also be used to establish lower bounds on the running time of algorithms and to analyze the complexity of geometric problems.

In summary, the principle of duality in computational geometry provides a powerful tool for relating geometric objects to their dual counterparts and for solving geometric problems by transforming them into dual problems. It has wide-ranging applications in various fields, including computer graphics, computer vision, robotics, and geographic information systems.

6.8 Describe the concept of quantum algorithms, and explain the potential impact of quantum computing on the field of algorithms and data structures.

Quantum computing is a rapidly growing field that has the potential to revolutionize the way we process information and solve problems. Quantum algorithms are a class of algorithms that take advantage of the unique properties of quantum mechanics to perform certain computational tasks much faster than classical algorithms.

One of the most well-known quantum algorithms is Shor's algorithm, which can factor large numbers much faster than any classical algorithm known today. This has significant implications for cryptography, as many encryption methods rely on the fact that factoring large numbers is a difficult computational problem. Shor's algorithm has the potential to break many of these encryption methods, which has spurred interest in developing new cryptographic techniques that are resistant to quantum attacks.

Another quantum algorithm that has received a lot of attention is Grover's algorithm, which can perform a search of an unsorted database much faster than any classical algorithm. This has applications in areas such as optimization, database search, and machine learning.

In addition to these specific algorithms, quantum computing has the potential to provide speedups for a wide range of computational problems, including simulation of quantum systems, optimization, and machine learning.

The impact of quantum computing on the field of algorithms and data structures is still largely unknown, as quantum computers are still in the early stages of development and are not yet widely available. However, researchers are actively exploring the potential applications of quantum algorithms in various fields and are working to develop new algorithms and data structures that are optimized for quantum computers.

Overall, quantum computing has the potential to greatly accelerate computation in many fields, and is an exciting area of research that is likely to have a significant impact on the future of computing.

6.9 What are persistent data structures, and how can they be used to model and manipulate data with history?

Persistent data structures are data structures that allow for the efficient retrieval and manipulation of multiple versions of the same data, representing its entire history. The key idea behind persistent data structures is that every time the data structure is updated, a new version is created, while the old version remains unchanged. This allows for efficient access to any previous version of the data, without having to copy the entire structure.

There are two main types of persistent data structures: partially persistent and fully persistent. Partially persistent data structures allow for efficient retrieval of any version of the data, but only allow updates to the most recent version. Fully persistent data structures, on the other hand, allow for efficient retrieval and updates of any version of the data.

There are many applications for persistent data structures, particularly in areas where maintaining a history of changes is important, such as version control systems, database management, and backup and recovery systems. Some examples of commonly used persistent data structures include persistent arrays, persistent trees, and persistent hash tables.

Persistent arrays are one of the simplest persistent data structures, and are essentially an array that allows for efficient retrieval of any previous version. In a partially persistent array, any previous version can be retrieved in $O(1)$ time, while updates can be performed in $O(\log n)$ time, where n is the size of the array. In a fully persistent array, both retrieval and updates can be performed in $O(\log n)$ time.

Persistent trees are another common type of persistent data structure, and are used to represent hierarchical data. Examples include binary search trees, red-black trees, and B-trees. In a partially persistent tree, updates can be performed in $O(\log n)$ time, while any previous version can be retrieved in $O(\log n)$ time. In a fully persistent tree, both retrieval and updates can be performed in $O(\log n)$ time.

Persistent hash tables are a persistent version of a regular hash table, which is used for fast lookups based on a key. In a partially persistent hash table, updates can be performed in O(1) time, while any previous version can be retrieved in O(log n) time. In a fully persistent hash table, both retrieval and updates can be performed in O(log n) time.

Overall, persistent data structures offer an efficient and flexible way to manage data with a history, and are increasingly important in applications where data integrity and versioning are critical.

6.10 Explain the role of streaming algorithms in processing massive datasets and provide an example of a widely-used streaming algorithm.

Streaming algorithms are used in processing data that is too large to fit into memory, or where the data is continuously generated and needs to be processed in real-time. The primary goal of these algorithms is to provide approximate solutions to various problems while using a limited amount of memory.

One example of a widely-used streaming algorithm is the Count-Min Sketch. It is used for approximate frequency counting of data items in a data stream. The algorithm creates an array of counters, and for each item in the data stream, it hashes the item to a specific index in the array and increments the counter at that index. The algorithm repeats this process for a fixed number of hash functions, and the final estimate of the frequency count for an item is the minimum value among the counters indexed by the hash functions. This algorithm uses a fixed amount of memory regardless of the size of the data stream and provides an approximation of the frequency counts with high probability.

Another example of a streaming algorithm is the Bloom filter, which is used to test whether an item is a member of a set. It works by creating an array of bits and a set of hash functions. For each item in the data stream, the hash functions are applied to the item, and the corresponding bits in the array are set to 1. To test whether an item is in the set, the hash functions are applied to the item, and if all the corresponding bits in the array are set to 1, the algorithm returns true. The Bloom filter provides a trade-off between the probability of false positives and the memory used to represent the set. The probability of false positives can be reduced by increasing the size of the array and the number of hash functions.

In summary, streaming algorithms are essential in processing massive datasets that do not fit into memory. These algorithms provide approximate solutions to various problems while using a limited amount of memory. The Count-Min Sketch and Bloom filter are examples of widely-used streaming algorithms that provide approximate solutions to the frequency counting and set membership problems, respectively.

6.11 Discuss the different types of parallel algorithms, such as data-parallel and task-parallel, and provide an example of a problem that can be solved using these techniques.

Parallel algorithms are designed to exploit the power of parallel processing architectures such as multicore CPUs, GPUs, and distributed computing systems. There are different types of parallel algorithms, depending on how the work is divided among the processing units.

One type of parallel algorithm is data-parallelism, where the same operation is applied to different subsets of data in parallel. This approach is well-suited to problems that can be decomposed into independent subtasks. For example, image processing algorithms that apply filters or transformations to individual pixels or regions of an image can be implemented using data-parallel techniques. Another example is the MapReduce programming model, which is used for processing large datasets in a distributed computing environment. In MapReduce, the data is split into independent chunks that are processed in parallel by different nodes in the cluster.

Another type of parallel algorithm is task-parallelism, where different tasks are executed in parallel. This approach is well-suited to problems where there are dependencies between different subtasks. For example, in a sorting algorithm, different subarrays can be sorted in parallel, but the final merging of the subarrays into a sorted array requires coordination and synchronization between the processing units. Another example is the parallel implementation of a graph algorithm, where different nodes or edges of the graph can be processed in parallel, but the overall algorithm requires coordination between the processing units to ensure correctness.

A widely-used example of a problem that can be solved using parallel algorithms is matrix multiplication. The standard algorithm for matrix multiplication has a time complexity of $O(n^3)$, where n is the size of the matrices. However, this algorithm can be parallelized using data-parallel techniques, where each element of the output matrix is computed independently. For example, on a GPU with many processing cores, the matrix multiplication can be split into smaller submatrices that are processed in parallel by different cores. Alternatively, the algorithm can be parallelized using task-parallel techniques, where different submatrices are computed in parallel and then combined into the final output matrix.

In summary, parallel algorithms are an important tool for solving computationally intensive problems by exploiting the power of parallel processing architectures. Data-parallel and task-parallel techniques are two common approaches to parallelism, each suited to different types of problems. Matrix multiplication is a widely-used example of a problem that can be solved using parallel algorithms.

6.12 Explain the concept of amortized analysis and its application in understanding the performance of data structures and algorithms.

Amortized analysis is a technique used to determine the average time complexity of an algorithm over a series of operations. It is a way to analyze the performance of data structures and algorithms that have a high variance in the time complexity of individual operations.

In traditional worst-case analysis, we determine the time complexity of the worst-case operation. This means that if there are n operations, the time complexity could be $O(n^2)$, even if most operations are much faster than that. Amortized analysis, on the other hand, looks at the average time complexity over a series of operations. This means that the time complexity of an individual operation could be higher or lower than the average, but the average time complexity over a series of operations will be more accurate.

There are three common methods of amortized analysis: aggregate analysis, accounting method, and potential method.

Aggregate analysis: In aggregate analysis, we analyze the total cost of a series of operations and divide it by the number of operations to get the average cost. For example, let's consider a dynamic array that doubles in size when it runs out of space. The cost of adding an element to the array is $O(1)$ on average. However, the cost of doubling the array is $O(n)$, where n is the size of the array before the doubling. If we perform n operations, the total cost is $O(n^2)$ in the worst-case scenario. However, if we use aggregate analysis, we can see that the total cost of n operations is $O(n)$, which gives us an average cost of $O(1)$.

Accounting method: In the accounting method, we assign a "charge" to each operation, which is greater than the actual cost of the operation. We then use this extra charge to pay for future operations. For example, let's consider a stack that uses an array to store elements. When the stack becomes full, we allocate a new array that is twice the size of the previous array. The cost of pushing an element onto the stack is $O(1)$ on average. However, when we allocate a new array, we charge each push operation an extra $O(1)$ to pay for the cost of the reallocation. We can show that the total charge is $O(n)$ for n push operations. Therefore, the average cost of a push operation is $O(1)$.

Potential method: In the potential method, we assign a "potential" to the data structure before and after each operation. The potential is a value that represents the extra cost of the current data structure compared to the best-case scenario. For example, let's consider a

binary counter that increments a number represented as an array
of bits. The cost of incrementing the counter is O(1) on average.
However, we can use the potential method to show that the worst-
case cost is O(log n). We assign a potential of 2^k to each bit
position that changes from 0 to 1. We can show that the potential
of the counter is at most 2n, where n is the number of bits in the
counter. Therefore, the average cost of an increment operation is
O(1) because the extra cost is paid for by the potential.

In conclusion, amortized analysis is a powerful technique for analyzing the average time complexity of algorithms over a series of
operations. It can be used to provide more accurate estimates of
the performance of data structures and algorithms than traditional
worst-case analysis.

6.13   Describe the concept of a compressed data structure and its applications in representing large datasets with reduced memory footprint.

A compressed data structure is a data structure that utilizes compression techniques to store and retrieve data more efficiently. Compressed data structures are often used to store large datasets in
memory or on disk, where reducing the amount of memory required
for storage is critical.

There are various techniques for compressing data structures, and
the choice of technique often depends on the specific application
and the characteristics of the data being stored. Some commonly
used techniques include:

Run-length encoding: This technique is used to compress datasets
that have long runs of repeated values. In run-length encoding, the
repeated values are replaced with a count of the number of times
they occur.

Huffman coding: This technique is used to compress datasets that
have varying frequencies of values. In Huffman coding, each value
is replaced with a variable-length code that reflects its frequency

of occurrence.

Delta encoding: This technique is used to compress datasets that have small differences between adjacent values. In delta encoding, each value is replaced with the difference between it and the previous value.

Bit packing: This technique is used to store a large number of small integers efficiently. In bit packing, the integers are packed into a sequence of bits using a fixed number of bits per integer.

Compressed data structures can be used in a variety of applications, such as:

Indexing large text corpora: Compressed data structures can be used to store the index of a large text corpus, allowing for efficient search and retrieval of documents.

Genome sequencing: Compressed data structures can be used to store large genomic datasets, enabling efficient analysis of DNA sequences.

Network traffic analysis: Compressed data structures can be used to store network traffic data, allowing for efficient analysis of network activity and detection of anomalies.

One widely used compressed data structure is the compressed suffix array, which is used to index large text corpora. The compressed suffix array is a compressed version of the suffix array, which is used to efficiently search for substrings in a text corpus. The compressed suffix array achieves compression by applying techniques such as run-length encoding and Huffman coding to the suffix array, reducing the amount of memory required for storage.

6.14 Explain the role of algorithmic game theory in understanding strategic interactions and decision-making in complex systems.

Algorithmic game theory is the study of algorithms and their applications in analyzing and designing strategic interactions among agents in a system. It lies at the intersection of computer science, game theory, economics, and operations research. Algorithmic game theory seeks to understand the strategic behavior of agents in various settings, including social networks, online markets, distributed systems, and decision-making scenarios.

One of the key concepts in algorithmic game theory is the notion of Nash equilibrium, which is a solution concept in game theory that captures the stable points in a game where no player can improve their outcome by unilaterally changing their strategy. A Nash equilibrium is a set of strategies, one for each player, where each player's strategy is the best response to the other players' strategies. Nash equilibria can provide insights into the behavior of agents in complex systems and help design mechanisms that incentivize agents to behave in a desired way.

Algorithmic game theory also encompasses the study of mechanism design, which involves designing rules and incentives that encourage rational agents to behave in a desired way. Mechanism design is often used in online auctions, voting systems, and resource allocation scenarios, among others. In mechanism design, the goal is to design a mechanism that maximizes social welfare or some other desirable property, while incentivizing agents to reveal their true preferences.

Some examples of problems that can be analyzed using algorithmic game theory include:

Ad auctions: Online advertising platforms use auctions to determine which ads to display to users. The auction mechanism needs to be designed to maximize revenue for the platform while ensuring that advertisers are willing to participate in the auction and bid truthfully. Social network analysis: Social networks can be modeled as games, where each user chooses which other users to connect with. The goal is to understand how users form connections and how network structure affects outcomes such as information diffusion and influence. Resource allocation: In scenarios where resources such as bandwidth or storage need to be allocated among multiple users, a mechanism needs to be designed that incentivizes users to reveal their true demands and distributes the resources in an efficient and fair manner.

In conclusion, algorithmic game theory provides a powerful framework for analyzing strategic interactions in complex systems and designing mechanisms that incentivize rational agents to behave in a desired way. Its applications are broad and include online markets, social networks, distributed systems, and decision-making scenarios.

6.15 Discuss the concept of self-stabilizing algorithms and their applications in fault-tolerant distributed systems.

Self-stabilization is a property of distributed algorithms that ensures the system will eventually recover from any transient fault and reach a correct state. In other words, self-stabilizing algorithms are designed to tolerate arbitrary initial states and any sequence of faults, regardless of their type or timing. This is an important property for fault-tolerant systems, where it is impossible to prevent all possible failures and the system must be able to recover from them on its own.

Self-stabilizing algorithms have applications in various areas, including distributed systems, communication networks, and real-time systems. Some examples of self-stabilizing algorithms include self-stabilizing spanning tree construction, self-stabilizing leader election, and self-stabilizing mutual exclusion.

A common approach to designing self-stabilizing algorithms is to use a combination of redundancy, synchronization, and error correction techniques. Redundancy is used to ensure that the system has enough resources to recover from faults, while synchronization is used to ensure that all nodes agree on the current state of the system. Error correction techniques, such as checksums and error-correcting codes, are used to detect and correct errors that may occur during the recovery process.

One widely-used self-stabilizing algorithm is Dijkstra's self-stabilizing token ring algorithm, which solves the problem of mutual exclusion in a distributed system. In this algorithm, each node in the system holds a token, which determines whether the node can enter its critical section. Nodes pass the token to their neighbors in a ring, and if a node that holds the token fails, the token will eventually be passed to another node, ensuring that the system remains in a correct state.

In conclusion, self-stabilizing algorithms are an important tool for designing fault-tolerant distributed systems that can recover from any sequence of faults. They use a combination of redundancy, synchronization, and error correction techniques to ensure that the system can recover from any transient fault and reach a correct state.

6.16 Describe the role of machine learning algorithms in optimizing and automating the discovery of efficient algorithms for solving specific problem instances.

Machine learning algorithms have been used to optimize and automate the process of discovering efficient algorithms for solving specific problem instances. This approach is known as algorithm design by optimization or algorithm selection by learning.

In algorithm design by optimization, a machine learning algorithm is trained to predict the performance of candidate algorithms on a specific problem instance. The performance metric may vary depending on the problem, but it could be the runtime, the memory usage, or the accuracy of the solution. The machine learning algorithm then generates new candidate algorithms by modifying the existing ones or combining them in novel ways. The performance of these candidates is evaluated, and the best ones are retained for the next iteration. The process continues until a satisfactory solution is found.

Algorithm selection by learning is a related approach where a machine learning algorithm is trained to select the best algorithm from a predefined set for a specific problem instance. The machine learning algorithm is trained on a set of training instances and their corresponding best algorithms. It learns to recognize the patterns in the problem instances that indicate the most suitable algorithm. The trained algorithm selector is then applied to new problem instances to select the best algorithm for each instance.

One example of algorithm design by optimization is the use of neural networks to generate sorting algorithms. Researchers have used neural networks to learn to sort arrays of different sizes and to generate novel sorting algorithms that outperform existing ones. Another example is the use of genetic programming to optimize the layout of printed circuit boards. Researchers have used genetic programming to evolve circuit board layouts that minimize the wiring length and hence reduce the manufacturing cost.

An example of algorithm selection by learning is the use of decision trees to select the best algorithm for solving a particular instance of the SAT problem. Researchers have trained decision trees on a large dataset of SAT instances and their corresponding best algorithms. The decision trees use the properties of the SAT instance to determine the most suitable algorithm for that instance.

In conclusion, machine learning algorithms can be used to optimize and automate the discovery of efficient algorithms for solving specific problem instances. These approaches have the potential to accelerate the development of algorithms and make them more accessible to non-experts.

6.17 Explain the concept of cache-oblivious algorithms and their applications in efficiently utilizing memory hierarchies in modern computer architectures.

Cache-oblivious algorithms are a class of algorithms that optimize for data locality without knowledge of the cache size or block size of a particular computer system. These algorithms are designed to work well on a wide range of memory hierarchies, including modern multi-level caches and disks, by using recursive subproblems with small subarrays that fit in cache, while minimizing the number of I/O operations.

One of the most widely used cache-oblivious algorithms is the cache-oblivious matrix transpose algorithm. The algorithm recursively partitions the matrix into smaller submatrices until each submatrix fits in cache, then transposes each submatrix in place, taking advantage of cache locality. The algorithm runs in $O(n^2/B + n \log\_BN)$ I/Os and $O(n^2)$ time, where n is the matrix size, B is the block size, and N is the cache size.

Cache-oblivious algorithms have also been developed for other problems, such as sorting, searching, and graph algorithms. For example, the cache-oblivious binary search algorithm is a modification of the classical binary search algorithm that recursively partitions the array into smaller subarrays that fit in cache, using the same strategy as the matrix transpose algorithm. The algorithm runs in $O(\log\_Bn)$ memory transfers and $O(\log n)$ time, where n is the size of the array and B is the block size.

Cache-oblivious algorithms have been shown to be competitive with cache-aware algorithms in practice, while providing theoretical guarantees on performance for a wide range of memory hierarchies. They are particularly useful for problems that involve large datasets that do not fit in main memory, such as in database management, scientific computing, and data analysis.

6.18 What is the role of algorithms and data structures in the design and analysis of bioinformatics applications, such as sequence alignment, genome assembly, and phylogenetic tree construction?

Bioinformatics is a field that combines computer science, statistics, and biology to analyze biological data, particularly in genomics and proteomics. In this field, algorithms and data structures play a crucial role in the design and analysis of various bioinformatics applications.

One of the main applications of algorithms and data structures in bioinformatics is sequence alignment. Sequence alignment is the process of comparing two or more biological sequences (such as DNA or protein sequences) to identify regions of similarity and differences. This process is essential for understanding the evolutionary relationships between species, identifying functional elements in DNA or proteins, and detecting mutations that may cause diseases.

There are different algorithms and data structures used for sequence alignment, including dynamic programming, heuristic methods such as BLAST (Basic Local Alignment Search Tool), and suffix trees or arrays. Dynamic programming algorithms, such as the Needleman-Wunsch algorithm, can find the optimal alignment of two sequences, but they are computationally expensive and not suitable for large-scale sequence analysis. Heuristic methods, such as BLAST, use indexing and filtering techniques to speed up the search for similar sequences but may miss some biologically relevant matches. Suffix trees or arrays are useful for searching for exact or approximate matches between sequences and can efficiently handle large datasets.

Another application of algorithms and data structures in bioinformatics is genome assembly. Genome assembly is the process of reconstructing the complete genome sequence of an organism from the short reads generated by sequencing technologies. This process involves solving computationally challenging problems, such as overlap detection, read alignment, and error correction.

Different algorithms and data structures have been developed for genome assembly, such as De Bruijn graphs, string graphs, and overlap-layout-consensus methods. De Bruijn graphs are used to represent the overlap relationships between k-mers (short sequences of length k) and can efficiently detect the presence of errors or variations in the sequence data. String graphs represent the reads as nodes and the overlaps between them as edges, allowing for more accurate reconstruction of the genome. Overlap-layout-consensus methods combine the information from multiple sources, such as reads and long-range sequencing technologies, to produce high-quality genome assemblies.

Phylogenetic tree construction is another important application of algorithms and data structures in bioinformatics. Phylogenetic trees represent the evolutionary relationships between different species or organisms based on their genetic or molecular data. Constructing phylogenetic trees involves solving complex optimization problems, such as maximum likelihood or maximum parsimony.

Different algorithms and data structures have been developed for phylogenetic tree construction, such as distance-based methods, maximum likelihood methods, and Bayesian methods. Distance-based methods, such as neighbor-joining, use the pairwise distances between sequences to construct the tree and are computationally efficient but may produce inaccurate results for complex datasets. Maximum likelihood and Bayesian methods use statistical models to estimate the evolutionary parameters and construct the tree, producing more accurate results but requiring more computational resources.

In summary, algorithms and data structures play a critical role in the design and analysis of various bioinformatics applications, such as sequence alignment, genome assembly, and phylogenetic tree construction. The development of efficient and accurate algorithms and data structures is essential for advancing our understanding of biological systems and diseases.

6.19 Describe the concept of multi-objective optimization algorithms and their applications in solving complex real-world problems with multiple conflicting objectives.

Multi-objective optimization is the process of optimizing a set of objective functions that may have conflicting or competing goals. This type of optimization is used in various real-world applications, including engineering design, finance, resource allocation, and many others. Multi-objective optimization algorithms aim to find a set of solutions that are optimal with respect to all objectives simultaneously, rather than just a single optimal solution.

One of the most widely used multi-objective optimization algorithms is the Non-dominated Sorting Genetic Algorithm (NSGA-II). This algorithm is an extension of the genetic algorithm and is designed to generate a set of Pareto optimal solutions, which are solutions that cannot be improved in one objective without sacrificing performance in another objective. NSGA-II sorts the population of solutions into different Pareto fronts based on their dominance relationships, and it uses selection, crossover, and mutation operations to generate new solutions that are biased towards the Pareto fronts.

Another popular multi-objective optimization algorithm is the Particle Swarm Optimization (PSO) algorithm. In this algorithm, each solution is represented as a particle in a high-dimensional search space. The particles move towards the Pareto optimal solutions by adjusting their position and velocity according to their own best-known position, the best-known position of the swarm, and the global best-known position. The PSO algorithm has been successfully applied to various real-world problems, including portfolio optimization, vehicle routing, and engineering design.

In addition to these two algorithms, there are many other multi-objective optimization algorithms that have been developed, including the Strength Pareto Evolutionary Algorithm (SPEA), the Multi-Objective Differential Evolution (MODE), and the Multi-Objective Simulated Annealing (MOSA). These algorithms differ in their underlying optimization techniques, their search strategies, and their efficiency in solving specific problem instances.

The development of multi-objective optimization algorithms has opened up new possibilities for solving complex real-world problems that involve multiple conflicting objectives. These algorithms provide decision-makers with a set of trade-off solutions that can help them to make informed decisions based on their priorities and preferences. Moreover, the use of multi-objective optimization algorithms can also lead to significant savings in time, resources, and costs compared to traditional single-objective optimization techniques.

6.20 Explain the role of algorithms and data structures in the design and analysis of network protocols, such as routing, congestion control, and security.

Algorithms and data structures play a crucial role in the design and analysis of network protocols. Network protocols are a set of rules and procedures that enable communication between different devices in a network. Efficient network protocols require fast and reliable algorithms and data structures to handle various tasks such as routing, congestion control, and security.

Routing protocols are responsible for determining the path a packet takes to reach its destination in a network. There are different types of routing protocols such as distance vector, link state, and path vector protocols. These protocols require efficient algorithms for calculating shortest paths and building routing tables.

Congestion control algorithms aim to prevent network congestion by regulating the flow of data through the network. These algorithms require efficient data structures for tracking the network's capacity and the amount of data being transmitted at any given time.

Security protocols aim to protect the network from unauthorized access and malicious attacks. These protocols require secure algorithms for encryption, decryption, and authentication, as well as efficient data structures for managing keys and certificates.

Examples of algorithms and data structures used in network protocols include Dijkstra's algorithm for calculating shortest paths, Bloom filters for efficient packet filtering, binary trees for efficient routing table lookup, and cryptographic hash functions for secure data transmission.

Overall, algorithms and data structures play a critical role in the design and analysis of network protocols, enabling efficient and secure communication between different devices in a network.

Made in the USA
Las Vegas, NV
01 February 2024

85182937R10089